D1612293

VOICES

FROM THE

GULAG

VOICES
FROM THE
GULAG

Life and Death in Communist Bulgaria

TZVETAN TODOROV

Translated by
Robert Zaretsky

THE PENNSYLVANIA STATE UNIVERSITY PRESS
UNIVERSITY PARK, PENNSYLVANIA

Library of Congress Cataloging-in-Publication Data

Voices from the Gulag : life and death in communist
Bulgaria / [compiled and edited by] Tzvetan Todorov;
translated by Robert   Zaretsky.

p.   cm.
Translated from the French ed.: Au nom du peuple;
original documents written in Bulgarian.
Includes bibliographical references and index.
ISBN 0-271-01961-1 (alk. paper)
1. Political prisoners—Bulgaria—Biography.
2. Concentration camp inmates—Bulgaria—Biography.
3. Bulgaria—History—1944–1990. 4. Concentration
camp—History. 5. Political persecution—Bulgaria.
I. Todorov,   Tzvetan, 1939–   . II. Zaretsky,
Robert, 1955–   .
DR93.A1V65   1999
365'.45'092—dc21
[b]   99-10414
                                                  CIP

First published in France as *Au nom du peuple: Témoign-
ages sur les camps communistes* © 1992 Editions de l'Aube.

English translation © 1999 The Pennsylvania State University
All rights reserved.
Printed in the United States of America
Published by the Pennsylvania State University Press,
University Park, PA 16802-1003

Contents

Foreword

In the last twenty-odd years I have read a hundred or more books on what has constituted the horror of our century: the presence of concentration camps. This has come about mostly through my contact with the *New York Review of Books,* whose editor has made it a custom to send me a large number of the books he receives on the subject, even though only a fraction of these titles is ultimately reviewed in the journal. My response to all of this material is not without a personal relevance. In 1944, I myself witnessed the Nazi terror in my native Hungary and was the object of mistreatment. Yet rarely, if ever, have I read such heartrending chronicles as the stories that appear in *Voices from the Gulag.* What makes the accounts of the former inmates of the Lovech concentration camp in Bulgaria so poignant is that they recount the experiences mostly of little people, among them apolitical youngsters who committed no greater crime than that of listening to Western "imperialist" pop music, or dancing the twist, or wearing tight trousers. Nor have I read many more abject apologies than those by the former torturers and killers of these harmless little people. The Communist police commanders and party functionaries who were guilty of these abominable crimes have not been punished, nor will they ever be.

The documents contained in this book are especially valuable because they deal with a country, Bulgaria, where the political purges, including massive executions, were more extensive and more cruel than perhaps in any other Soviet Bloc country. Between 1944 and 1989 there existed nearly a hundred concentration camps in Bulgaria, of which Lovech was not even the most important. In other Communist countries, the number of camps tended to decline following the death of Stalin in 1953, so that by the years 1959–62, which is the period discussed here, Hungary, for instance, had no more concentration camps, only prisons for political defendants. Prison inmates have been sentenced; they have a reasonable chance to be released at the expiration of their term. Inmates in the camps have never been sentenced and thus have no idea when, if ever, they will be set free. In Bulgaria, the Gulag system continued for many years after the death of Stalin; it was as if the party leadership and the political police had become demented. Consider that, whereas in "fascist" Bulgaria no Jewish citizen was killed for being Jewish and from Bulgaria proper no Jews were handed over to the Germans, in Communist Bulgaria Jewish prisoners were handled with particular brutality.

The value of these documents is further enhanced by the fact that their compiler and editor and the author of the extensive introduction is Tzvetan Todorov. This Franco-Bulgarian philosopher, political thinker, and historian, whose *Facing the Extreme: Moral Life in the Concentration Camps* (Metropolitan Books, 1996) is perhaps the most significant recent work on the concentration camps in Hitler's Germany and Stalin's Soviet Union, is well qualified to present these documents to us. A foremost intellectual who experienced Communism in his native Bulgaria, Todorov approaches the subject with understanding and goodwill. He explains the differences and similarities between the Communist and the National Socialist systems and aptly discusses the Communist New Class's perceived need to set up concentration camps, less for the true enemies of the regime, who were being dealt with in the courts, than for the apolitical innocents. The goal was to inject fear into the rest of the population. But, unlike *Facing the Extreme,* which argues that indestructible moral standards and deep humanity were preserved by many inmates in even the worst Nazi and Soviet camps, the voices in the present work evoke an almost unmitigated sadness. This sadness speaks to the absurdity of the situation in a country that, in the early 1960s, had an obedient population, nurtured no expansionist ambitions, and was threatened by no one.

Of the many interesting passages in the Introduction, I find one of the most revealing to be Todorov's reference to the indifference, even hostility, of the population in the area around the Lovech concentration camp. This is all the more important because some historians have drawn significant ethical and political conclusions from the callousness with which the inhabitants of German, Austrian, and Polish towns near the great Nazi concentration camps viewed the inmates of those camps. Todorov shows that such behavior has less to do with political and racial prejudice than with the terror and collective brutalization characteristic of totalitarian regimes. I agree wholeheartedly with Todorov that the camps were not a perversion but the essence of both Communist and Nazi systems. I also agree with Todorov that punishing the guilty is a hopeless proposition today. The best that can be done, though it is not being done, would be to unmask and, through the activities of "truth commissions," to humiliate the perpetrators. Rather than save the Communist system, these people actually hastened its demise.

In the famous 1957 Billy Wilder film *Witness for the Prosecution,* Marlene Dietrich, playing a manipulative and ruthless German woman, complains to Charles Laughton, who plays a formidable attorney, that, because of her accent, she would not be believed in a British court. "My dear ..."—Laughton protests in righteous indignation—"in our courts we will accept the evidence of witnesses who speak only Bulgarian and who must have an interpreter; we accept the evidence of deaf-mutes, who cannot speak at all, as long as they tell the truth." Bulgaria is indeed a faraway country, at least from the British and American, although not from the Russian or the Turkish or the Greek, point of view. Its culture is as vibrant as that of any European country, with the distinction that sufferings in Bulgaria during the twentieth century have been on the Balkan, and not on the Western European, scale.

The American public, which has what seems an insatiable—and justified—interest in Holocaust reports, needs to be reminded of the crimes of other regimes as well. This is especially so in order that Americans not develop a smug attitude, for example, that "such things could not happen here." The World War II internment of the Japanese Americans was a comparatively mild affair on the scale of international brutality in that period, but the earlier killing

of Native Americans often matched in thoroughness the more re-
fined and more extensive practices of the twentieth-century tyrants.
It is necessary to remind the public that no determined regime has
ever found it difficult to recruit volunteers for torture and murder.
Worse yet, the vast majority of citizens everywhere prefers to remain quiet at times of crisis and danger: not to risk anything for
anyone is the usual reaction. Those who have faced the agonizing
moral choices inevitable under an oppressive system know how few
are the truly brave and the truly just. Yes, it could happen even here.

István Deák
Columbia University

Translator's Preface

I wish to thank the following individuals and institutions, who have made this translation possible. Dr. Ted Estess, the Dean of the Honors College at the University of Houston, furnished important moral and material support; the Office of Sponsored Programs at the University of Houston and its director, Ms. Rosemary Grimmet, provided an important travel grant at a critical moment; and my colleagues in the Department of Modern and Classical Languages, Dr. Harry Walsh and Dr. Claudine Giacchetti, helped greatly on the issues of translation and transliteration. Keith Monley has been exemplary in the policing of my language; and Peter Potter at Penn State Press has, once again, gracefully balanced the often conflicting demands of friendship and editorship. My friend Maika Haddad welcomed me at his home in Paris while I worked on the translation. I was introduced to Tzvetan Todorov a few years ago by our mutual friend Adam Zagajewski. The meeting led to this translation, as well as to the beginnings of a European education; I have been very fortunate to spend time in the company of these remarkable men.

Tzvetan Todorov has kept a close watch on my translation, as well as on the transliteration of names, from the Bulgarian to the French to the English. Any errors that remain are mine alone.

Preface

Soon after the fall of Todor Zhivkov, in 1990, the newly born and adversarial press in Bulgaria began to publish accounts on the Communist concentration camps. They also published interviews with former guards and commanding officers. More detailed accounts subsequently appeared, most notably *Belene*, by Stefan Bochev (1990); *Kutsian*, by Yordan Vŭlchev (1990); *Prisoners in Their Own Land*, by Georgi Zhechev (1991); and, most recently, the collection *Witnesses: The Bulgarian Gulag* (1991). These works have added to an older literature that had been published in the West and that includes *Belene*, by Nedyalko Geshev (1983).

In 1990, Bulgarian television broadcast a four-and-one-half-hour-long documentary film called *The Survivors (Stories from the Camps)*, written and directed by Atanas Kiryakov. Dealing with Bulgaria's concentration-camp system, the film is based on a series of interviews, conducted by the director, with various individuals who either worked or were interned at the camps. A few years after the film's successful release in Bulgaria, an abridged version was shown on French television.

The present work is the result of an initiative taken in Sofia by the literary agency Medium. They placed at my disposal the transcript of the film, along with several published works that treat the subject of the concentration camps. They also asked five individuals (Boris Gikov, Nikolas Dafinov, Bozhidar Petrov, Nadya Dunkin, Jacqueline Doncheva) to provide additional recollections for use in the present volume. I have tried to retain the heart of these previously unpublished accounts, while adding important passages from the film or other Bulgarian works on the camps, for which references are provided in the footnotes.

My special thanks to Nikolas Dafinov, Vasil Stanilov, Atanas Kiryakov, and Rositsa Gurkovska.

Introduction

Not so long ago, in an empire that had seemed impervious to all change, history suddenly lurched forward. Over the course of two brief years—1989–91—old regimes in Eastern Europe collapsed, and radically new problems arose in their stead. Social, ethnic, and national tensions replaced the former confrontation between "Communism" and "capitalism." The rapidity of change and urgency of new problems tempt us to turn this page of history and focus entirely upon the present difficulties. It is, after all, natural that the more recent the hardship, the greater the claim it has on our attention. But this impulse ought to be resisted.

Human reason and passions have not changed for thousands of years, yet we continue to be amazed by the events taking place in front of our eyes. Just as great writers allow us to unearth hidden features of human nature, so too does historical change reveal facets of social life whose existence we had never before suspected. In this respect, the historical events that have just taken place are exceptional. Unlike their colleagues in the natural sciences, students of human societies do not, as a general rule, have access to experimental methodology. Instead, they are limited to studying what already exists. Yet for the better part of our century, a significant percentage of humanity was subjected to an unprecedented experiment: they were condemned to live under totalitarian regimes. These experiences, though deeply distressing, also offer a crucial lesson about the political animal we call man. It is a lesson not only for the peoples who lived under these regimes but also for those Westerners who were more or less passive observers of this experiment. For those of you comforted by the strange names or circumstances, beware: these events could have happened in your own countries. Indeed, they still can.

This book is devoted to the effort to better understand and judge the totalitarian experiment in its Communist guise. It focuses on an institution I consider to be both essential to and symbolic of totalitarianism: the concentration camp. We will examine its nature through the accounts of those whose lives came into contact with it: the former inmates and their families, as well as those who guarded them. I wish to emphasize that the intent of this work is neither polemical nor accusatory. Of course, concentration camps still exist in those countries where Communist regimes remain in power—Vietnam, China, North Korea, Cuba—and it goes without saying that they must never be tolerated. But in the former Soviet Union and Eastern Europe, such camps belong to the past: it calls for little courage to denounce them. The urgency of combat has passed, and it is now equally urgent to understand and reflect.

Realizing this goal is the point of this book. Rather than provide factual information, it seeks to provoke reflection on the fate of fellow human beings trapped in the mechanism of totalitarianism. The factual historical record of this phenomenon is being established by others; I am instead interested in the fundamental historical experience of the men and women who passed through these camps. As a result, I decided it was legitimate to narrow the focus of this book to Communist Bulgaria, where both totalitarian rule in general and the concentration camps in particular seem to have functioned in an exemplary fashion. Similarly, from the nearly one hundred camps that existed in Bulgaria during this period, I have chosen to concentrate on the camp at Lovech, which operated from 1959 to 1962. (A few pages in this collection, however, do make reference to experiences in other camps.)

On the other hand, I have sought to present this single example as fully as possible. It was not too long ago that Lovech was open for business, serving as a lightning rod for the greatest excesses of the Communist terror. It has, as a result, sparked a number of detailed testimonies. These accounts deal not only with the years of imprisonment but also with life before and after the camp. They also reveal how the entire country bears the brutal stamp of the concentration-camp system. Recorded here are not only the voices of the former inmates but also those of their kapos, guards, officers, and even an interior minister. However, I prefer not to focus exclusively on the nearly intolerable accounts of torture in the camps. Though death is considered to be the great leveler, men also tend to resemble one another when subjected to the extremes of cruelty. The questions that hedge this phenomenon—the who, why, and how—are to my mind more compelling.

Though the exemplary character of Lovech justifies the narrow focus of this book, I must confess to another reason. I am the same age as the witnesses who speak in the first part of this book. Like many of them before they were arrested, I lived in Sofia during the very same period: 1959–62. Frequenting the same places as they did, I was guilty of the same "crimes": I wore the same clothes, listened and danced to the same music, repeated the same jokes, and felt the same way about the police. These witnesses evoke a world—with its taboos and its tricks, its admirable and contemptible individuals—all too familiar to me.

I was an adult and did not turn a blind eye to all that surrounded me. Yet the fact remains: that horror was part of my world, but I did not know that this camp existed. I was unaware of it and hence did nothing to combat it. I know that this was not completely fortuitous: I belonged to a privileged class that, to a certain degree, sheltered me from the "troubles" that others knew. I am not now seeking to escape my guilt, since I know that I have nothing in particular for which I ought to feel guilty. Nevertheless, because of these aforementioned coincidences, I will never be able to say that these stories do not concern me.

One last preliminary word: the participants in this book are not professional writers. In fact, most of their words were not written, but spoken; this book contains the transcriptions. Many of them had their education cut short, and they may sometimes appear heavy-handed or clumsy. These accounts, however, give voice to a truth so powerful that the reader is overwhelmed.

TOTALITARIAN SOCIETY

The study of the totalitarian experience is hampered by a specific difficulty: namely, the continuous interaction, or collision, of the totalitarian ideal (more or less explicitly proposed, more or less consciously acted upon) with the real world. As a result, it is difficult, if not impossible, to view the totalitarian project in its pure state. Even the most zealous of its agents must take into account human psychology and the play of existing economic and political forces, resulting in a compromise between the totalitarian ideal and the reality of the world. It is the same imperative of compromise that also explains the historical evolution of totalitarian regimes. Nevertheless, the study of the totalitarian project must not be dismissed with the excuse that it has never been fully realized. To the contrary, it is only after the ideal has been identified that its reality, itself infinitely more complex and changing, becomes fully intelligible. Hence, I shall first discuss the blueprint of totalitarianism, rather than its actual construction with its train of partial and contingent changes.

Totalitarianism can be—indeed, has been—described from a number of angles: philosophical and political, economic and sociological. Rather than choose among these various perspectives, I shall instead try to place myself inside the minds of the subjects of a totalitarian state and see the regime through their eyes. This psychopolitical approach emphasizes group psychology and its relation with politics. The analysis is based on the testimonies found in this book, as well as other and older accounts. I shall also make use of my own experience under a totalitarian regime.

The regime had for us three essential characteristics. First, it claimed that it operated according to a Communist ideology. Second, it used terror to control its population. Lastly, life under this regime was governed by personal interest and the will to power. These characteristics are, I believe, necessarily separate, distinct, and irreducible. As a result, I prefer not to use the term "Communism," which corresponds to only the first of these three traits. Instead, the term "totalitarianism" equals the sum of all three parts and, equally important, allows for the possible appearance of a different ideology from that of Communism (as was the case with Nazism).

Let me now define the key words that inform my approach to

totalitarianism. The first is "ideology." The intellectual antecedents of a perfect society on earth—one that is proposed as the goal for one's own imperfect society—are diverse and distant. Most notably, there are the traditions of Christian millenarianism, Renaissance utopianism, and, closer to our own time, early socialist thought. It is perfectly legitimate to add to this list the name of Karl Marx. The founder of the Communist movement is, after all, responsible for the major economic and social ingredients of the Communist doctrine.

When one lives in a totalitarian society, one tends to underestimate the importance of ideology. It seems to be little more than empty words and window dressing, disguises and lies, that haven't the slightest relationship with the real world. "They" tell us about the radiant future in order to make us forget the grim present, and "they" evoke the power of the people so as to hide their greed, personal wealth, and privileges. Moreover, one cannot but notice that the content of the official ideology, or at the very least the interpretation of its axioms, continuously shifts. At the same time, this ideology is held to be unchanging, since its truth is unquestioned. Two of the more obvious examples, taken from the realm of foreign affairs, are the evolution of Soviet Communism's relations with Hitler's Germany at the end of the 1930s and that with Maoist China during the 1960s. There are, of course, many other examples.

However, the interference produced by the regime's lies and doublespeak risks obscuring the actual function of ideology. First of all, certain areas of society are, despite the need to compromise with the real world, governed by ideological principles. This often is the case with the management of the Communist economy: for instance, by the collective pooling of the means of production or farming, or by the primacy given to heavy industry. This also explains the invariably disastrous results of these same economies, governed by their fidelity to the broad, abstract principles of Marxism. Most important, however, the recourse to ideology—regardless of its content—is an essential ritual. Totalitarian countries may well be under the thumb of a single individual or ruling caste, but if this were to be openly acknowledged, it would entail their disappearance. This point is critical. Ideological discourse is like an empty shell, but without that shell, the state would collapse.

"Terror" is my second term. Who was the first to discover that daily doses of terror could be used to govern a people? That terror could bend an entire population to one's will? The answer is less obvious than it is with the "discoverer" of the Communist ideal. Thomas Hobbes arguably prepared the ground by identifying the fear of death as the first and most basic of human emotions. If such is the case, those who followed Hobbes might well conclude, why not take advantage of it? A form of state terrorism appeared during the French Revolution, while in the mid-nineteenth century the Russian revolutionaries Tkachev and Nechaev outlined a systematic use of terror. In his *Dialogues philosophiques*, Ernest Renan reasoned in a manner that anticipates the totalitarian use of terror. In order to guarantee absolute power in a century when atheism reigns, Renan wrote, it is no longer enough to hold the mythical threat of hell over the heads of a rebellious population. Instead, one must create a "real hell"—a concentration camp—to break the will of the rebels and intimidate the rest of the population. He also proposed the creation of a special police force, formed by amoral agents devoted to serving the existing power structure. They would be, in Renan's words, "obedient machines prepared to commit any enormity." At the beginning of our own century, Georges Sorel also reflected upon the legitimacy of violence.

However, credit for systematizing these ideas, then putting them into practice, undoubtedly belongs to V. I. Lenin, the father of the first totalitarian state, and his Bolshevik comrades. It was Lenin who laid down a few simple principles. First, anyone who refuses to submit to the state is the state's enemy. Second, enemies of the state deserve just one fate: elimination. "Our enemies," Lenin announced, "must be exterminated without pity." A potent side effect of this treatment is the intimidation of the rest of the population. As Trotsky noted, the revolution must be conducted as if it were war: by "killing a handful of individuals, we will frighten thousands of others." Third, the perpetration of terror is controlled by a specific institution, which at the time was called the Cheka. As its first director, F. E. Dzerjinski, observed, "Our organization reaches everywhere. The people fear us." Finally, the institutionalization of the terror is justified by a warlike vocabulary. Hence the Bolsheviks spoke of "class struggle" and "dictatorship of the proletariat."

The totalitarian state cannot live without enemies, and they in turn are terror's raison d'être. Should there be no enemies, they must be invented. And once the enemy is identified, the response is swift and pitiless. As the first of the great Soviet authors, Maxim Gorky, declared in a brutal formula: "If the enemy refuses to surrender, he must be exterminated." This task is, at the outset, facilitated by dehumanizing the enemy. "Vermin" and "parasite" are a couple of the usual labels applied to the enemy. (The Nazis proceeded in a similar fashion with the Jews and their political enemies.) This is why the camp guards at Lovech could assert, "We Communists are proud to kill the enemy" or "Subtracting an enemy adds a loaf of bread." Certain incurable and hereditary traits make one a state enemy. For example, a former resident of the concentration camp will always be first in line for a return visit, and the children of the class enemy—be it the bourgeoisie or its rural equivalent, the kulaks—are no less inimical to the state than were their parents. Once an enemy, always an enemy. The status of being an enemy is not just chronic but also infectious: the friends, wives, or husbands of enemies are, by their very proximity, vulnerable.

Once the terror has been installed—that is, once the people know that the threat of death or repression is not mere verbiage—society changes dramatically. It is a harsh truth to observe that the society has never existed in which man spontaneously rejoices in the happiness of his fellow man. To the contrary, one man's misery makes for another's joy. Montaigne described this form of *Schadenfreude* as "the malignant delight we take in the suffering of others." The means to make the other suffer—to exercise terror—is within the reach of everyone in a totalitarian society. In fact, one is encouraged and rewarded for taking advantage of this opportunity. All that is required to damn my fellow human beings—my boss, my assistant, my rival, my neighbor, my brother—is to point them out to the relevant officials of the Party or Bureau of State Security (whose jurisdictions overlapped). The branded individuals will henceforward either be denied promotion or fired, find themselves deported to the provinces or imprisoned in a camp. In the end, some of them will be murdered. As one former inmate remarks, "Anybody could for whatever reason send whomever they wished to their doom." The great innovation of totalitarianism is that extreme evil is available to anyone.

Though the ideological foundations of Nazism and Communism are very different, they both resort to the machinery of terror. Certain writers underscore the fact that, under the Nazis, the Jews were pursued, not for what they *did,* but for what they *were:* Jews. But this was also the case with Communism, which insisted upon the repression—or, at times of crisis, the extermination—of the bourgeoisie as a class. One did not have to *do* anything in order to be branded: membership in this class alone sufficed. The children of bourgeois parents, moreover, bore the same mark of infamy. The Gestapo outstripped the Stasi in its brutality and cruelty, but the latter affected more individuals. In East Germany, there were approximately one hundred thousand permanent agents, two hundred thousand contract employees, and about one million part-time collaborators in a population of some ten million men and women.

The third and last trait of totalitarianism is the reign of self-interest. The reality of everyday life under totalitarian regimes obviously has little in common with official twaddle. Instead, life follows principles that are shaped by a relentless pursuit of the biggest slice of the cake. Scratch the regime's ideological facade and you will find self-interested cynicism and the will to dominate one and all. Self-interest of course exists under other forms of government. Yet it is with totalitarian regimes that it attains its greatest strength. Indeed, the totalitarian system cannot be understood if this is not taken into account.

Neither Marx nor even Lenin was responsible for inventing the reign of self-interest. It has instead become associated with Communist regimes since Stalin's taking of power. This second phase of the Soviet state corresponds to the form of totalitarianism found in postwar Eastern Europe. We know that Stalin rapidly liquidated the entire Bolshevik old guard—the very individuals, in other words, who still believed in ideas. As a result, the model Communist was no longer a fanatic, but instead an *arriviste*. He was prepared to change his convictions without hesitation, for he aspired to personal success and power, not the distant victory of world Communism. Marx, Lenin, and Stalin were the three fairy godfathers who bestowed these virtues upon the totalitarian state while it was still in its cradle.

The establishment of this way of life corresponds to a concept of man and society whose genealogy can easily be traced, even if the principle of self-interest was never consciously admitted. One might cite the French materialists of the eighteenth century, such as Helvétius, who argued that self-interest was the sole motivation of human action. Nietzsche's psychological insights are similar. He wrote, for example, that "[e]very physical body seeks mastery of space and the extension of its strength (the will to power), repelling any obstacle in its way." This observation offers a fairly precise description of the hidden and open struggles that the various agents of totalitarian society must engage in. It is revealing, in this regard, that a number of observers of Soviet society have been struck by Stalin's greater fidelity to Nietzsche than to Marx.

How must an ordinary man go about increasing his power? He has one option: try to join the Party, place himself under those already in positions of power, and devote himself to his tasks with total submission and great industry. If he succeeds, he will soon have earned minor material privileges. More important, he will enjoy a number of symbolic advantages and find himself with greater power over others. He will be able to advance or obstruct their careers, even influence the very unfolding of their lives. Should he rise higher in the Party hierarchy, he will have access to new privileges: country homes, luxury apartments, official cars, access to special stores, trips abroad. And should he rise to the very top of the state and Party bureaucracies, he will influence the lives of millions of human beings. On the other hand, if he fails to be admitted into the Party, all is not lost: the path of betrayal and denunciation is still open. This will allow him, if only on a sporadic basis, to enjoy the exercise of power over others. Totalitarian society is thus a *pseudo-ideological dictatorship*. Each of these three traits is an essential ingredient, and their interaction divides the population into several distinct groups. At one extreme is the *nomenklatura:* those individuals who belong to the various bureaucracies (the Party, state, police, and army) and enjoy various privileges. At the other extreme are the declared or potential enemies of the regime, chosen according to their personal activities or their membership in a certain group. Between these two extremes is the great bulk of the population, who are subject "only" to those inconveniences common to one and all.

According to its ideology, Communist society is classless. This is partly true, though hardly for the reasons found in Communist dogma. Instead, it is because the groups just described resemble more closely the caste system in certain traditional societies than the class system of nineteenth-century capitalism. The principal difference between these groups is not economic, as is the case in capitalist societies. Since the state is essentially the sole employer, everyone works for the same firm. As is the case with castes, the differences are, in the broadest sense of the word, political. The differences between these castes consist in the distribution of a certain number of rights and privileges. Though Communist countries claim to respect the principle of equality, it is observed only in the breach: it is difficult to conceive of all the ways in which one's life is controlled by the politics of privilege. One example is education: not everyone has the right to go to the university or school of one's choice. So, too, with housing: apartments (which are always in short supply) are distributed according to an array of political and social criteria. As for the provisioning of food and staples, there are special stores for members of the Central Committee and yet others for members of the Political Bureau. Trips abroad are forbidden to some and limited to fraternal Communist countries for others; there are those who have access to foreign currency, while others are denied such access. Even traffic patterns are not exempt: certain streets are open to everyone, while others are limited to a select few.

These new castes have a great deal in common with traditional castes. For example, both display complex and detailed hierarchies. Each of the three principal castes—nomenklatura, state enemy, and everyone else—is subdivided into several clearly defined subcastes. Becoming a Party member is only the first step, since one can be promoted to the Central Committee, followed by the Political Bureau (substitute and full members, secretaries and vicesecretaries). The power of an ordinary policeman is eclipsed by that of the political police. In Bulgaria the latter was called the Bureau of State Security, and those who worked for it wielded tremendous power. But even State Security was eventually bypassed by a third police force known as the UBO, a veritable aristocracy of repression whose primary task was to keep an eye on the political police. Similarly, just as with traditional castes, membership is hereditary: the children of the privileged orders inherit the same privileges, and the practice of endogamy—that is, marriage within the same group—perpetuates caste identity. This explains the natural evolution of such societies to a monarchical transmission of power: Ceausescu's wife, Brezhnev's son-in-law, Kim Il-Sung's son, Zhivkov's daughter were all anointed as successors to the head of state.

Nevertheless, the new castes in Bulgaria were distinguished from the traditional castes by the possibility of moving between castes. Though this mobility, which they shared with social classes, was not easy to negotiate, it did exist. On the one hand, you could slide down the ladder. This was the case for those veterans of the resistance who, because they remained honest men, were stripped of those privileges that distinguished them from the masses. In certain cases, they actually became "enemies" of the state and were subjected to deportation. On the other hand, you could make your way up the caste system. You might be promoted from the category of "enemy" to the relative safety of the masses; one day, you might even reach the prized goal of the nomenklatura. Totalitarian society, like democratic societies, is the opposite of traditional cultures: it is an intensely competitive world fueled by personal ambition. Provided that you are firmly grounded in the rules of the game, it is even possible to start at the very bottom and finish at the top of state power.

Promotion is simple: you must be willing to serve your superiors and to inform on everyone else. Denunciation is not a transient character flaw: it is basic to the structure of totalitarian society. For those in power, it assures that nothing escapes their gaze. But since the entire population has to be watched, the number of state agents is never sufficient. As a consequence, society must be compelled to watch over itself. For the general population, this offers a means of advancement: to slander one's fellow is not only a source of immediate satisfaction in that you decide another's destiny, but it is also an efficient way to eliminate a rival. Consequently, it hardly matters whether the denunciation is a sheer lie or contains elements of the truth (which is not improbable, since no one can be entirely satisfied with the regime). Doing harm to those around you is the one criterion. But denunciation is a sword accessible to everyone, and this may create a problem, the denunciator being himself the possible target of a denunciation. As a result, networks of support and mutual aid inevitably appear as a means of rescue at critical moments.

As for servility, it is the dues paid to one's superiors. It is neither a coincidence nor an accident that personality cults have existed in all Communist countries. Writers and intellectuals showed themselves to be especially inventive in singing the praises of those in power, which explains their often intimate ties with heads of state. But this phenomenon extends to one and all, for all bootlickers eventually pocket certain favors. The only limit is that imposed by rival groups and individuals. The widespread practice of denunciation and servility explains the general decay of moral values, as well as the flourishing of cynicism in totalitarian societies.

If one were to look for a common denominator to all totalitarian societies, it would be their hostility to the autonomy and dignity of the individual human being. Autonomy and dignity are experienced when one behaves according to one's own decisions and will. The often illusory nature of this belief, along with the fact that we are influenced by unconscious forces or economic and social factors, is irrelevant. Our sense of dignity is founded upon the interpretations we offer for our acts, and our very humanity begins with the possibility to refuse, to resist, to say no. Yet everything about a totalitarian society—and the very term "totalitarian" is revealing in this regard—aims to prevent the individual's autonomy, which is based on the possibility of being the source of one's own decisions. In a totalitarian world, the most highly rewarded of virtues is docility, and the least tolerated of principles is liberty.

Totalitarian doctrine deliberately privileges the group over the individual and provides the means for controlling the individual by depriving him or her of all economic autonomy. Hence the hostility toward private property and the impulse to nationalize industries and collectivize farms. This also explains the great care taken in the indoctrination of children (through their schooling and extracurricular activities), reflecting the state's desire to challenge family solidarity, which is a potential source of autonomy. Similarly, the spouses of "enemies" are strongly urged to divorce their partners, for here, too, individual choice must give way to that of the state. Terror strikes all of those who dare disagree. One of the most unforgivable of errors is humor—telling of political jokes, or simply having a sense of humor. Humor is a mark of distance from authority, and thus a proof of individual autonomy. It is for this same reason that totalitarian regimes do not welcome fanatics, for they may one day follow their ideals rather than official orders. A totalitarian regime instead rewards those bureaucrats who have proved their loyalty through a succession of moral and political betrayals.

At first glance, the individual's renunciation of autonomy seems to clash with the will to power that is encouraged in totalitarian societies. However, when society is nothing more than the theater for the confrontation of individual wills, one must always be prepared to surrender to those stronger than oneself. Indeed, one can only climb the ladder of political power by displaying one's docility. Individuals who live in democratic societies must accept from the outset the limits imposed on their desire to dominate, and agree to the rules of a multiparty system based upon consensus and the toleration of minorities. This is the price to be paid for the ability to enjoy a life of autonomy within these societies. In totalitarian societies, on the other hand, there are theoretically no limits:

everyone can aspire to total domination over everyone else. As a result, the confrontation of wills threatens each and every one with defeat, and as in an athletic contest, the losers are more numerous than the winners.

Totalitarian society constitutes a coherent and, as history has shown, viable whole. Its efficacy is beyond question: human beings cringe when terror is unleashed and bend when constraints are imposed. In a country like Bulgaria, the initial postwar phase of totalitarian repression was so brutal that there was no "dissidence" for the next thirty years. Yet over the course of two short years— from 1989 to 1991—these same regimes were erased from the map of Europe. How did this miracle take place? Internal causes, not external pressures, appear to have led to the collapse of this empire. (The rare pressures from the outside never mortally threatened Communism, even if the "Star Wars" initiative had a certain impact.) Communism's ultimate collapse revealed the existence of cracks in the structure. But what precisely were the causes that undermined the basis of these societies?

First of all, it seems clear that totalitarian society contains tensions that might be labeled structural. I have already remarked upon the ambiguous role that ideology plays, being simultaneously indispensable and unnecessary. In order to be effective, terror must be absolute, yet only ideology can legitimize a totalitarian regime. When cynicism replaces faith, the appearance of faith must at least be saved—hence the emphasis upon ritual. But ideology frays once it becomes a mere formality, a ritual that inspires disbelief. When ideology is no longer able to fill its role, terror relaxes and dissidence takes root. A similar contradiction can be seen in the will to power. The latter is simultaneously cultivated and forbidden; it is the ultimate motivation, yet even the most powerful individuals must be prepared to abandon it at any moment. One eventually discovers that it is more profitable to play according to the rules of democracy, which entail a partial renunciation of personal ambitions but guarantee that advantages already won will not be lost.

More generally, one might also argue that the death of totalitarianism in Europe was hardly due to the fact that it was not "good": an unjust society can endure indefinitely. Rather, totalitarianism failed because it was not "true." In other words, it was based on notions of human nature and society that we know to be false.

Most observers, for example, very quickly perceived the baselessness of the Communist hypothesis concerning the economy. A fully centralized and planned economy is doomed to failure. This is why Communist regimes were periodically forced to resort to NEP-type economic policies, which repudiated the very principles of Communism.[1] But the regimes were also periodically forced to punish the desire for greater wealth, for it inevitably led to a desire for greater autonomy. In this respect, Nazism, which at least had the good sense not to allow its ideology to dictate its economic program, proved to be more effective than Communism.

Anthropological or psychological hypotheses may reveal a more important, though less obvious, reason for the collapse of Communism. It is at best debatable that human beings "naturally" aspire to be free. One could, in fact, argue that totalitarianism's attraction, unconsciously felt by most of us, is born from the fear of liberty and responsibility. As Erich Fromm affirms in his book *The Escape from Freedom,* this partly explains the popularity of all authoritarian regimes. Nevertheless, the desire of modern Europeans (though not necessarily those who belong to traditional societies) to exercise their autonomy and insist upon their liberty of choice cannot be gainsaid. As a result, the submission required of the individual by the totalitarian state cannot indefinitely be maintained. Plants can be forced to grow horizontally, but the moment the pressure is relieved, they reassert themselves and begin growing upward. A person may well be so frightened that he will never again wish to raise his head, but the "education" of repression must start from scratch with this individual's child, or even his neighbor.

It is equally poor psychology to limit oneself to the Hobbesian

---

1. Translator's note: The New Economic Policy (NEP) was a series of market-oriented reforms introduced by Lenin in the mid-1920s in order to spur industrial and agricultural production. These reforms were eventually suppressed by Stalin.

and Nietzschean vulgates, which claim that society is the "natural" battlefield of all against all and that each individual seeks only to extend his or her power at the expense of others. This is tantamount to a hyperindividualist view of humankind, which affirms the self-sufficiency of the individual, with the corollary that "others" are simply obstacles to eliminate or rivals to defeat. This is a dangerous illusion: it is the gaze of the other that validates our own existence and recognizes our individual value. It is thus essential to attract the benevolence of "others"—a dynamic for which terror clearly is insufficient. Our desire to be esteemed and respected by strangers is as great as our desire to be loved and cherished by family and friends. No one could ever seriously maintain that this could be accomplished by the use of force.

Equally erroneous is the hypothesis, found in Helvétius and Nietzsche, that morality is "artificial," a hypothesis that reduces morality to mere submission to societal convention or compares it to a mask that hides our individual greed and ambition. This is simply not true. The sentiment of justice is born within us spontaneously and freely. It may be dormant for years, but it is easily awoken. This is at the source of the events that unfolded in 1989. The totalitarian regime foresaw everything except one thing: the appearance of a head of state who, listening to the dictates of his conscience rather than his own interests, forbade the shooting of rebelling demonstrators. On this day the bell tolled for the Communist regime, and its perhaps unwilling gravedigger was named Mikhail Gorbachev.

By attributing the collapse of Communist totalitarianism to truth's ascendancy over error, we can find reason not to despair. But do not confuse this with finding reason to be optimistic. After all, the Communist regime maintained itself in power for several generations—a simple yet sobering observation when we realize that each of us has just one life to live. Still, when all is said and done, we can affirm that the worst is neither inevitable nor irreparable: something in human nature prevents humanity from destroying itself forever.

AN INSTITUTIONAL CORNERSTONE: THE CONCENTRATION CAMP

The concentration camp is doubly emblematic of totalitarian regimes: it is both a part of the whole and an image of the whole. First, it is the very cornerstone of these regimes, for it incarnates the "real hell" described by Renan and is more effective than death itself in the implementation of state terror. Second, the camp is the quintessence of totalitarianism in that the society is run according to the same, though somewhat diluted, principles as run the former. A society in which concentration camps are no longer conceivable cannot qualify as totalitarian.

Every society necessarily designates a place where it imprisons those who have broken its laws. But it is essential to know if such imprisonment is the result of a judicial or an administrative process, and if it leads to prison or to concentration camp. In Eastern Europe, as in Nazi Germany, it was the administration (the police) that made use of the camps, while the courts had recourse to the prisons. This is a crucial difference, and was justifiably underscored by David Rousset, a French survivor of Buchenwald who led the protests in the 1950s against the Soviet concentration camps. Those who were sent to these camps were never charged or sentenced. Instead, the police decided who was to be imprisoned—an arbitrary act justified by a special law. There was a specific reason for this: the purpose of the camps was not to punish those guilty of crimes—that is, individuals who were judged and imprisoned—but to terrorize the population by their indiscriminate use. Prisons are built for those who are judged and found guilty, while camps exist for the innocent.

Needless to say, Communist justice was usually a mere parody of justice. There were, for example, the famous show trials mounted in the 1930s under Stalin, which then served as models for the trials of the 1940s and 1950s in Eastern Europe. Moreover, life in some Communist prisons, where torture and murder were common currency, was hardly enviable. But the fact remains that individuals who experienced both prison and camp speak almost nostalgically of prison. It is telling that those few who succeeded in escaping a concentration camp often committed a minor crime immediately after in order to gain the security of a prison. Judicial procedures in Communist regimes may well have been mere formalities, but they were better than nothing: the prosecution had to offer evidence against the accused, while the defense sometimes dared to reveal the inanity of the charges. As wicked as the law might have been, a law it remained, engaging both the prosecuting authority and the defendant. And as terrible as jail may have been, it nevertheless was governed by rules that one could respect, and therefore preserved some degree of basic human dignity.

The concentration camp, on the other hand, imposes a far harsher regime, founded upon forced labor. At Lovech, for instance, the prisoners worked in a quarry, breaking and loading stones. If only hard labor had been the worst of it, however! Far more terrible was the fact that the prisoners' torment was tied to the arbitrary character of their fate. Never having been formally judged, they never knew how long they would be in the camp. Six months? Ten years? The rest of their lives? Not having been sentenced to any form of legal punishment, how could they know what was in store for them? They were simply put in the hands of torturers whose intentions were impenetrable, though clearly hostile. Each camp cultivated its own form of destruction. Buchenwald is known for its starvation diet and diseases; Kolyma took advantage of the winters and sheer fatigue. The Bulgarian camps, especially Lovech, were distinguished by the most primitive form of torture: beatings with clubs and sticks. There was no rule or principle, even the most absurd, that could earn your liberation or even a simple improvement in your living conditions (which might in turn save your life). Everything depended upon the mood of the person who stood in front of you, armed with a club and heavy with hatred, driven by the sole desire to make you suffer. Dependence upon the capricious will of one individual is worse than life under the most rigorous of laws.

Who, exactly, were sent to the camps? Officially, at least, the answer is simple: enemies. But since any and all actual enemies—

never numerous to begin with—had already been condemned, imprisoned, or shot, the concept of "enemy" had to be revised. We can shed light on this issue by considering, not the official documents, but rather the lives of those who had been imprisoned. Paradoxically, the totalitarian state needs enemies, the very species it has eliminated. Since they have been rendered extinct, enemies are perforce created by the state. To understand this logic better, the category of "enemies" can be subdivided into three classes: opponents, nonconformists, and rivals.

Opponents are those whose political opinions differ from the official Party line. They are, in short, a true "opposition." In the countries of Eastern Europe, one can distinguish three waves of opposition. The first wave consisted of those people who belonged to the "old regime," many of whom were compromised by their collaboration with the Germans. This opposition was eradicated in the aftermath of the war. The second wave was made of the non-Communist antifascists who, naive enough to join with the Communists in 1945, were then eliminated before 1948. The third and last wave included the internal Communist opposition from 1949 (the rupture with Tito) to 1953 (the death of Stalin). This group was usually identified by the litmus test of "defense of national interests or loyalty to the Soviet Union." While the principal figures in this opposition were systematically liquidated, their followers, families, and collaborators were sent to the camps. The common trait linking all these individuals was the fact that they had expressed disagreement with the official party line, even if they never behaved as enemies or threatened those in power. They were "opponents" whom the state transformed into enemies. A plurality of opinions is intolerable for a totalitarian state, and every disagreement must be immediately crushed.

Nonconformists form the second class of enemies. In Bulgaria, they were infinitely more numerous and provided the bulk of the camp population. The flow of prisoners from this category never dried up, even though one cannot properly speak of an opposition in Bulgaria after 1950. Though this group did not actually combat the party line, it failed to support the party with sufficient ardor. Worse, these individuals gave proof of a mild degree of autonomy. Large sections of the population were guilty of such non-conformism, including those peasants who may have grumbled when forced to join the new farming cooperatives, to which they had to surrender their only horse or cow. Or all of those who sold used goods or worked on their own. Thanks to this stubborn persistence in earning their own livelihoods without becoming state employees, they were labeled idlers and con artists. Or practicing Christians. Or homosexuals. The label was even applied to kids who got into occasional fights (the category of "hoodlum" was one of the most flexible for the regime).

Certain variations in the use of the term "nonconformism" deserve special attention. The term could be used literally and applied to individuals whose values and behavior diverged from the accepted norm, even if the relationship of this norm to official politics remained mysterious. Take fashion, for instance: young men who wore tight pants and young women in short skirts were given a couple of warnings, then packed off to a concentration camp from which they might never return alive. Music even slightly akin to jazz or rock and roll was immediately suspect, since it came from the West. This was also true for any dance introduced after the tango. One witness, who was a filmmaker at the time, remembers being arrested and judged in 1964 for dancing the twist. The man avoided being sent to a camp, but the reasons adduced for the condemnation are revelatory: "[W]e are not against modern dances, but recognize that there are two ways to dance: the Western or capitalist way; and ours, the socialist way." Extramarital sexual relationships were marks of moral turpitude and could lead to deportation as well. Information concerning such affairs was systematically used as a means of blackmail.

Contact with foreigners was another favorite charge that justified repression. To associate with foreigners, be they on assignment or on vacation, athletes or businesspeople, was always suspect, since it encouraged espionage. But it was no less dangerous to admire objects that came from the West (in official parlance, "to devote oneself to the adulation of imperialist technology") or to study foreign languages such as French, English, Italian. (Spanish was removed from the list of suspects following the victory of Communism in Cuba.) You were also branded if you had a preference for reading "Western" authors. In short, a potential traitor required no less vigilance than an actual traitor.

The slightest expression of protest could lead to camp. One fellow was packed off because, while waiting in the interminable line at the bakery one day, he grumbled, "Grain for Moscow, straw for us." Another, surprised by a relatively well-stocked counter, joked, "Fresh bread? Is it election day already?" Numerous individuals were deported or imprisoned for having retold anecdotes about the heads of the Party or state or Our Friend, the Soviet Union. Another was deported because he shared news heard on the BBC with a neighbor (a crime labeled "broadcasting rumors harmful to the state"). Yet others were persecuted who, though having committed not even a minor crime, were not subservient enough. They proved reluctant, for example, to denounce others or to show sufficient enthusiasm during a parade or in an obligatory labor brigade. Hence the charges brought against one woman in a letter of denunciation: "She behaves arrogantly and gives herself airs around others. She doesn't choose her social circle according to the new socialist morality." Every form of autonomy—economic, social, moral—had to be broken.

The last class of inmates (which was numerically unimportant) consisted of rivals of more powerful individuals, for whom internment was a convenient form of elimination. This was the consequence of placing the machinery of repression within the reach of one and all. The accounts below include the case of a divorced woman who, having won enough money in a lottery to buy an apartment, was denounced by her ex-husband, a policeman, who had her sent to a camp and then took over the lodging. Or the wife who had chanced upon her husband with another woman and made a public scene, after which her husband, who happened to be a military officer, rid himself of his intolerant wife by having her deported. Or, again, there was the man who tried to defend his daughter against the advances made by the Party secretary of the village and was sentenced to five years in camp. Or the woman who rejected the propositions made to her by the local head of a People's Organization and was also sentenced to five years.[2] Or simply consider the neighbor who grumbles that your house casts a shadow on his. He happens to have a brother who works in the Ministry of the Interior, and so the next thing you know, you are packed off to camp without the time to pack your bags. All of this would be laughable did it not illustrate a fundamental trait of totalitarian societies: the ease with which one can transform a rival, or anyone who bothers you for any reason, into an enemy and recruit for a concentration camp. Once you were identified as an "enemy," the consequences were simple: if, following an initial warning, you did not quickly adopt the life of absolute servility, you would be arrested, beaten (if a man), and bundled off to camp.

How was the everyday life of a camp inmate organized? In March 1962, an inquiry commission arrived at Lovech, led by Boris Velchev, a member of the Political Bureau. A veteran of the Bulgarian resistance, this commissioner had himself been imprisoned during the war in a camp run by the fascist regime. Also, over the several preceding months, the quality of life at Lovech had been greatly improved, and the majority of inmates had been released. Nevertheless, Velchev was so shocked by what he saw that, even thirty years later, he had not forgotten: "The living conditions in the fascist camps were much better. I was overwhelmed."

The camps were run by teams of officers from the political police. These men all had more or less the same social profile: the offspring of poor rural families, they joined the Communist resistance at an early age. After the war, they were quickly promoted and were educated in Party schools (that were sometimes located in the USSR). They owed everything they had to the Party and were devoted to it body and soul. They did not bother about ideas—clichés replaced actual thought—and they zealously executed the orders they received from above. The very notion of questioning orders never

2. Translator's note: The Communist Party created various organizations according to profession, age, sex, neighborhood and so forth, and used them to organize and control the population.

crossed their minds. Fairly crude and of average ability, they showed no sign of either imagination or compassion. It is not surprising that most of them—though there were exceptions, and a few actually resigned—had sadistic tendencies: they were placed in a situation of total liberty and might even be promoted for their harsh treatment of the prisoners. As a result, they surrendered themselves to the perverse pleasure that comes from controlling another's life—a life upon which one can inflict pain, a life that one can simply extinguish. In other circumstances, they would not have behaved sadistically. Quite simply, they were ordinary men and women who had discovered a convenient way to enjoy the prerogatives of power.

They were supported in their work by subalterns and, most important, the "brigade chiefs." These men, who were either common criminals or subservient political convicts, oversaw the work details. They were the equivalent of the kapos in the Nazi camps and used clubs as a means of persuasion. They were the ones who usually beat the prisoners to death.

A day in the lives of prisoners at Lovech might proceed as follows: During the morning roll call, the chief of police (assigned to the camp by the Bureau of State Security) would choose his victims. It was his habit to pull a small mirror from his pocket and show it to them: "Here, take a look at yourself for the last time!" Every condemned man was then given a bag, which would be used to bring his corpse back to camp that same night. They had to carry the bags themselves, just as Christ carried his cross upon Golgotha. They left for the work site, in this case a rock quarry. Once there, they were beaten to death by the brigade chiefs and dropped into the sacks, each of which was then tied by a piece of iron wire. That evening, their comrades brought the bags, which had been thrown into a hand cart, back to camp, where they were tossed behind the latrine. As a measure of economy, the sacks were carted off by a truck only when twenty had accumulated. Those inmates who escaped this fate but who failed to meet the daily quota of rock were singled out during the evening roll call: the police chief traced a circle in the dirt and pummeled with his stick those who were ordered to step inside.

All the elements of this extraordinarily harsh regime—the superhuman work quotas, the relentless beatings, the execrable living conditions—had a single goal: to shatter the prisoner's inner resistance. If you did not submit, you died; if you did submit—if you were obedient and silent—you might survive. The slightest trace of autonomy was erased; the last measure of dignity was demolished. Here is one survivor's description of the prisoner's daily lot: "At dawn you were brutally torn from the sole moment of authorized rest, and for the rest of the day, from the darkness of daybreak to the darkness of sunset, you were on your feet, always moving, never allowed to sit or lie down, in a state of constant and continuous stress, starved and thirsty, beaten and physically exhausted. All the while, to prevent you from finding rest and consolation in your thoughts, the whip constantly snapped over your head, while filthy insults and commands from the guards rang in your ears."[3]

The only way to better one's lot was to collaborate with the authorities. Former "opponents" were required to sign a declaration in which they solemnly renounced their previous political views. Anyone could aspire to become an informer or even brigade chief. But few did so—not out of heroism or a spirit of resistance, but because of a kind of resignation. Moreover, there was a pervasive fear that everyone internalized, leading them to submit with little or no protest. The prisoners rarely spoke to one another, since they had neither the time nor the strength. As one prisoner recalls, "So much time passed without exchanging a single word with another person, that I'd talk to the wall just to make sure I could still speak." They did not complain and, quite justifiably, were not ashamed of their complete submission. Whoever bends does not break: there was no other way to survive. According to another inmate, "I said nothing, so that I might survive to see my son. Sooner or later the slave returns home, but no one returns from the tomb." In this regard, this book includes a remarkable document: a prisoner's first letter to his parents. It is a complex mix of self-accusation

3. Georgi Zhechev, *Prisoners in Their Own Land* (in Bulgarian) (Sofia, 1991).

and humility, pain and expectation of the horrors that were in store for him, love for his family and his attachment to life. The guards had achieved their goal, but so too had the prisoner.

This treatment reached well beyond the prisoners, affecting their family and loved ones. As one of the camp officers observed at the time, "Though the parents of those who were killed were always notified, there's not a single case where they complained or asked about the cause of death." Even if this were true, it certainly does not prove that the individuals concerned believed that justice had been done. In reality, the repression was so brutal that no one risked complaining. They knew that they would be next: "I was called and told that my brother had died. I didn't dare ask how. I didn't want to suffer the same fate." One judge recalls that all complaints were made orally and were never written down. Thirty years later, the former prisoners still hesitate to speak about their experiences. "I have children to think about. . . . Ask someone else."

The camp's neighboring population did not sympathize with the inmates. First of all, it was far easier to believe what the authorities said about the prisoners. One thus avoided a guilty conscience for overlooking occurrences of injustice. Moreover, it was simply more prudent to mind your own business: by keeping away from those stricken by the plague, you were less likely to be contaminated. Local administrators thus persuaded themselves to take advantage of this free labor, since it was provided by hardened criminals anyway. One farmer whose house was just outside the camp insists even today, "I saw nothing, heard nothing, and can say nothing." This is how it was, is, and would be tomorrow if history repeated itself. Let's not fool ourselves—heroism has never been in abundant supply.

This intimidation of the entire population was, of course, an essential part of the regime's overall project. The camps were kept secret, and no one knew exactly what was going on behind the barbed wire—apart, that is, from those individuals directly implicated. At the same time, however, rumors concerning the camps spread. The very mention of their names stirred fear, as they were meant to do. In fact, were we to view the camp as the crystallized essence of the entire state, we would conclude that the camp was to the country what the blow of a club was to the head of a prisoner: a reminder of the proximity of terror. And just as no one could escape the camp, no one could escape the country, also surrounded by barbed wire, without risk of being shot.

During the late 1980s, Communist propaganda in Bulgaria tried to present the reality of the camps differently. It would point to the fact that, following an official inquiry, a certain camp was closed by the Party leadership. This was offered as proof that the camps were a perversion of official policy rather than its logical climax. But a closer look reveals that the camps were never completely shut down. For every camp that was closed, two were opened; inmates were freed in May, only to be arrested again in September. (In fact, the camps in Bulgaria existed as late as the 1980s, despite official declarations to the contrary. They were used to imprison members of the Turkish minority.) Moreover, the regime's suppression of the camps was not followed by any significant or formal disavowal. Despite the crimes committed in these camps, there were no judicial proceedings against the perpetrators, and those who ran the camps were instead later decorated and promoted.

Finally, and most important, the Communist dictatorship repressed the population in ways that were milder than, but of the same essential nature as, the management of the camps. For example, there was the practice of deportation to or house arrest in isolated areas of the country. This was no less an instance of purely administrative punishment than were the camps, and was aimed at potential (though less dangerous) enemies and occasionally their families. Overnight, one would be stripped of work or a place to live, forbidden to stay in one's hometown, and forced to move to a distant village. There one would work the soil, subjected to the local despot's whims and forced to report every day to the local police station. Instead of deportation, any suspect individual could be saddled with countless suspensions of privileges and rights: forbidden to live here or to work there, denied medical care in one place or refused admission to a school in another place, or even kept from seeing this or that person. And there were yet other forms of intimidation: physical attacks by mysterious "thugs," mail censorship, telephone wiretaps, slander and persecution. A concentration camp the size of an entire country could not sustain an unrelenting flow of terror. Nevertheless, the men and women who ran it had a variety of methods to advertise the state's potential to unleash terror, and to remind the population that no one, no matter how small, could escape its reach.

A BITTER HARVEST

The camps are closed today, and the Communist Parties, where they still actually exist, have been reduced to the political opposition. But the traumas of the past remain with us. How are we to come to terms with this chapter of history?

One rather simple answer could be formulated in practical terms. Every society has a duty toward its past, guaranteeing that it not be erased or forgotten. Yet, in the name of civil peace, certain voices from the former Communist countries have called for a collective forgetting of the past. These individuals, focused exclusively on the short term, are trying to erase the traces of acts that only now appear to them as crimes. In doing so, they have succeeded in damning themselves: their labeling of historical researchers as "vultures" and "necrophiliacs" simply confirms the presence of corpses. They are guilty of perpetuating a politics of secrecy and defending a centralized control of information, both of which are characteristic of totalitarian regimes (in which the activity of the political police was justified by "state secrets"). Now the repression of the past, laden as it is with explosive material, is as dangerous for the group as for the individual. If the past is ever to be overcome, it must first be spelled out. No obstacle must stand in the way of truth. The open dissemination of information, which has always been the most effective weapon against concentration camps and totalitarianism in general, must now be allowed to shield us against any potential recurrence. It is imperative that the state and Party archives be preserved and that historians, regardless of their ideological persuasion, be granted free and open access. This is the one and only way to reconstruct the past in all of its complexity.

Absolute access is the one fundamental rule that must be followed, and if it is to benefit the entire society, ordinary citizens must be included. As in the case of Germany, it is necessary to guarantee all citizens free access to the archives during a clearly determined period of time (for example, twenty years, after which prescription applies). Of course, one runs the risk of discovering that friends were actually informers, yet even such horrifying revelations are better than suspicion and doubt.

But there is more at stake than duty toward history and memory. There is also a duty toward the protagonists of these past events. Many are still alive and known to one and all. What attitude should be adopted toward them? As for the victims, the task is straightforward. Those who are dead—either summarily executed, beaten to death, or killed by the harsh treatment in the camps—must be honored as are those killed in battle. Those who fled their country must be cleared of all suspicion, and their rights must be fully restored. Those deported to the camps must be financially compensated for all the wrongs done to them. Though such gestures will never efface past suffering, they will invest the past with moral significance and lighten the sense of having been the victim of an absurd injustice.

The responsibility of the torturers and executioners raises more difficult questions. This has already been revealed by the experience of denazification, yet there is an important difference: in the absence of a militarily victorious Allied camp, each of the former Communist countries is on its own in coming to terms with the past. The problem this presents is illustrated, almost to the point of caricature, by the accounts of those who worked in Bulgaria's concentration camps. No one, regardless of his or her role in this kingdom of terror, feels guilty for what occurred. The murderous kapos pretend to have been the mere tool of their superiors. The camp officers insist that they were the simple executors of camp regulations and ministerial directives. The vice-minister of the interior, who was directly responsible for the running of the camps, and the minister himself affirm that they simply obeyed instructions from the Political Bureau, the Council of Ministers, and ultimately the Party leader. And though the explanations of the party leader do not appear in this book, he has elsewhere insisted that he was not responsible for the excesses, perversions, and mistakes of his subordinates. Not only did he or his close collaborators never kill anyone, but they were unaware that the deportees had been turned over to sadistic madmen, who alone were responsible for these errors. He also asks us to remember the historical context—tense class struggle, threats from abroad, and so forth—that we might better understand the state of mind that allowed such excesses to occur.

Responsibility keeps shifting up the hierarchy, like a time bomb passing from hand to hand. Once it reaches the top of the political ladder, it is immediately dropped to the bottom of the ladder, and the game starts all over again. In short, I'm not guilty, the other guy is.

This defense strategy is by no means accidental; it faithfully reflects the very structure of what we can call totalitarian crime. As opposed to traditional crime, totalitarian crime is never committed by someone acting alone. First of all, there is a radical separation between those who make the decisions and those who execute them. In this way, the former keep their hands clean, while the latter keep their consciences unruffled. Decision-making bodies are subdivided into several smaller units, spreading responsibility across a large number of agents. At the highest rungs of the ladder, the interior minister proposes the building of new camps, which he thinks translates the wishes of the first secretary. Yet the first secretary insists that he gladly would have done without the camps, but that the interior minister forced his hand. As for the lowest rungs of the ladder, the guard who clubs a prisoner on the head during the morning roll call is not trying to kill, but only doing his job. The guard who finishes the prisoner off at evening roll call in turn claims that he acts out of the charitable desire to end the victim's suffering. Standing between these two extremes is a vast bureaucracy dedicated to transforming the concrete horrors of the camps into mute statistics, and translating the abstract orders given by the highest reaches of the state into the rules of everyday life. Responsibility is divided among the various agents of the state, each of whom assumes a specific task, with the result that no one bothers over either the principles or actual consequences of their actions. In this way, no useless questions need to be asked. This is what underpinned the efficacy of the totalitarian machine back then and now guarantees the agents' sense of impunity.

Along with the fragmentation and dilution of responsibility caused by the long chain of command, a second important obstacle impedes the court's pursuit of the former torturers and executioners: they acted in the name of the law. Apart from certain excesses and actions beyond the call of duty, these individuals obeyed not only their superiors but the law as well. As for the acts of sadism, many of them were committed in the early years and have since fallen under the statute of limitations. In order to respond to this double difficulty, tribunals along the lines of Nuremberg (or the trial of Klaus Barbie in France), charged with trying individuals accused of crimes against humanity, have been proposed for the former Communist countries. Were such courts to be instituted, the defense of having obeyed the law, as well as any existing statute of limitations, would become null and void.

Without entering the details of the debate over crimes against humanity, I do not find such a solution to be very desirable. The concentration camps and the forms of violence that they allowed, indeed cultivated, were not a perversion of the totalitarian system; they were an essential element, a logical consequence, a crystallized expression of that very system. Those who ran the concentration camps were no less consistent and no more excessive than those who ran the nation's industries or its smallest villages. In the end, it was chance that led the totalitarian state to assign the work of repression to certain individuals and management policy to others. The latter were no less ignoble or malevolent than the former. The totalitarian state is all of a piece: one element cannot be condemned, while others are exempted. Yet, at the same time, one cannot condemn all the agents who worked on behalf of a state that lasted some forty-five years. Were criminal charges to be multiplied to this degree, any effort at punishment would be rendered impossible.

What then are we to do? Should we quickly declare a general amnesty and act as if all the cats of the deep totalitarian night were equally gray? We know all too well that this was not the case, and we would wrong not only the surviving victims but also the very idea of justice were we to renounce judging acts of such enormity.

New problems call for new remedies. Apart from the relatively straightforward case of those crimes that remain liable to prosecution and can be tried according to current laws, totalitarian crimes committed under the former Communist regimes bear more closely upon the collective conscience of the nation than upon the demands of justice. I can readily imagine the creation of a special jury to which nationally respected individuals would be named and whose judgments would be broadcast to the entire nation. Empowered to establish the degrees of political responsibility, the jury would also pronounce sanctions affecting the honor, rather than the civil liberties, of those found guilty. (Were condemnations to prison involved, they would lead to immediate pardons, given the advanced age of most of those involved.) It is intolerable that those in charge of the concentration camps—this scourge of humanity—should still enjoy the decorations, the symbolic and material privileges, and indeed all the civil rights of their country. By the term "those in charge," I do not mean the killers and thugs, or even the ruthless officers of the Bureau of State Security, who ruled the camps and who will always haunt the memories of the survivors. The term instead applies to the political chiefs whose faces the victims never saw and whose names they often never even knew: the members of the Political Bureau, the ministers of the interior, the central headquarters for the camps. What is essential is not to punish X or Y, but instead to reestablish the ideas of truth and justice in a land where they had been flouted for nearly half a century.

Up to now, I have only considered the legal and practical measures that must be taken if one is to come to terms with one's past. But even these measures, should they be taken, will not fully resolve the problem. The law is not designed to control a people's past, and numerous consciences will still be haunted by memories long after judgments have been rendered. The totalitarian experience—with its paroxysm, the concentration camps—was a collective trauma for those who lived through it, and one does not heal a trauma of this magnitude overnight. As David Rousset aptly remarked in a Paris courtroom in January 1951, "The enormity of the camp is not due to the fact that people suffered and died in it, but to the fact that people experienced it. It was in the camp that the prisoner suffered complete self-degradation; it was in the camp that the men who guarded this prisoner also suffered complete self-degradation. A country that permits the existence of concentration camps is rotten to the core. No one is left untouched in such a world, and there lies the greatest misfortune we can ever know."

Though the tumor has now been removed, the body still bears the scars of totalitarianism. We must never pity the former executioners as much as we should the former victims, yet they too are to be pitied. The souls of those who participated in this repressive system will forever be blighted. They first had to numb themselves to any emotion that might have troubled their consciences. Yet they must today convince themselves—for their own sake as well as the sake of their families—that no evil occurred under their watch and that they have no reason to feel guilty. The countless informers and bootlickers were often caught between a rock and a hard place: they had no birthright in the privileged caste, and worse yet, they often had some flaw known to the organs of the Party and for which they had to pay. Is there anyone in a totalitarian society who has no cause for reproach? Only the person who has never lived in such a world could make such a claim. As Vaclav Havel has observed, the mark of totalitarian dictatorships, as opposed to traditional dictatorships, is not that a minority represses a majority, but that we are all, in various ways, made complicit in the mechanism of repression. Everyone becomes, if only to a minor degree, both the object and subject of the regime, both executioner and victim.

Having physically recovered, the former victims still bear the emotional scars of their previous life. The simplest temptation for them is to give in to the desire for revenge and inflict on their former torturers the same pain that they themselves had experienced. But this simple reversal of roles would mark yet another victory for totalitarianism. No one has yet proposed that the camps be reopened, this time to punish the former guards and their superiors; nevertheless, I recently read in an anti-Communist Bulgarian newspaper an editorial that offered an assessment of the former leaders of the camps: "Humanitarian principles were never meant to apply to those people who lost their human dignity and soiled our world." This phrase is a pure product of totalitarian thought, yet have we the right to criticize its author? After all, where and when could he have learned to think differently? During the years of Communist dictatorship, prisoners would sometimes encounter in a different camp or work site their former guards, whose privileged status had ended with the closing of their camp. It appears the settling of scores did not go much beyond the exchange of threats and the occasional fistfight. All the more reason today, when the torturer's actions are more distant but the victim's power much greater, that this earlier serenity and equity be reaffirmed.

A more hidden temptation may well be the enduring desire to identify with the victim. During the years of persecution, the former inmates were thought to be enemies, not victims. It was only with the reestablishment of justice that yesterday's enemy has become today's victim. Yet the status of victim has its advantages: along with a few material compensations, it entails an enviable symbolic standing. The former victims have the unlimited right to claim and proclaim their rights, and a certain form of self-gratification is assured once this status is assumed as one's identity. We all know people who, in their private lives, would happily surrender the satisfaction of their desires for the right to complain endlessly over their dissatisfactions. It is no less the case for public life, where the official status of victim guarantees a certain convenience. But such a role ultimately corrupts those who assume it. The reign of justice is infinitely preferable to that of injustice, but neither guarantees the possession of moral virtue. An act is not morally virtuous if the subject who performs it is also the one who benefits from it.

Given that the concentration camps were society in minia-
ture, it is not surprising that similar problems occurred in seemingly
distant and unrelated areas. For example, not very long ago, in the
domain of scientific research, ideology was privileged over scientific
criteria, since loyalty to the Party was more important than actual
results. The path of least resistance today consists in simply revers-
ing the contents of the ideology while keeping intact its container.
Where it was once an advantage, membership in the Communist
Party is now a handicap, and those now in leadership roles in the
world of science are the most vociferous anti-Communists, though
not necessarily the best qualified (though they have the same excuse
that was previously expressed by the offspring of the working class:
"The regime prevented me from performing better and proving my
excellence!"). But, once again, should we be outraged? Where could
these individuals have learned a higher form of moral virtue? It is
clear that such behavior is not the result of newly restored health, but
instead reflects the aftereffects of the illness. The most appropriate
and probably the most difficult way to learn from this tragic experience would be to cast a critical eye on oneself rather than the other.

In the accounts that follow, we discover that certain prisoners
have had the courage and wisdom not to recount all that they experienced during this traumatic period. If they had told everything,
one survivor observes, their children would have been forced to
play forever the role of parents. The parents thus decided that a
certain amount of ignorance was, if not bliss, at least preferable.
They, however, did not forget what had happened, and when the
right moment arrived, they found the words to express it. But
they did not allow the past to be confounded with the present, or
to keep it under its control. The individual mourns in a similar manner: the dead are not forgotten, but they are treated differently
from the living. They are still loved, but their presence is no longer
always missed. The recovery of the past is critical for a people. But
it must not be transformed either into an object of obsessive interest
or a mere tool of political protest and demands; this would only lead
to an endless cycle of revenge and reprisal (the history of the
Balkans offers a good example of the disasters sparked by a strictly

literal approach to memory). Instead, by reflecting upon past injustices, we can draw lessons for the future and perhaps restore the very ideal of justice.

But are we capable of giving ourselves over to the labor of mourning and reinterpreting the past? Traumatic experiences are sometimes indelible and insurmountable. In a documentary film devoted to the concentration camps, a woman recounts the following story: "The day after my father's first arrest, a policeman came to our house around noon and gave my mother a summons to appear at five o'clock that afternoon at Police Station No. 10. My mother, who was a very pretty and sweet-tempered woman, put on a dress and left for the station at the designated time. The three children waited and waited. She finally came back at 1:30 the next morning, white as a sheet, her clothing rumpled and her hair disheveled. She walked immediately to the woodstove, opened the lid, and, having undressed, threw all of her clothing inside the opening. She ran a bath and took us in her arms. We then went to bed. The following morning she tried to kill herself. It was the first of three attempts. She then poisoned herself two times. She's still alive and lives with me ... she is mentally ill. We've never been able to learn what it was that they did to her."

The exact nature of the crime committed against this woman matters little. It took place in the fall of 1944, and though she is still alive, she will never recover. As with this mother still haunted by hallucinations, the population of half a continent suffers from physical and mental problems from which they may never be freed. Who will take care of them? The world will absorb this disaster as it has absorbed past disasters, all the while preparing for those yet to be born. As for the individuals, they will carry their wounds to the grave.[4]

4. Translator's note: Tzvetan Todorov has published several books that deal more extensively and systematically with some of the issues and ideas evoked briefly in this introduction. In particular, see his *On Human Diversity* (Cambridge, Mass.: Harvard University Press, 1993) for the intellectual background to totalitarian regimes; *Facing the Extreme* (New York: Henry Holt, 1996) on the function of concentration camps in totalitarian societies; and "The Abuses of Memory" (*Common Knowledge*, 1996, 1) on the uses of memory.

Historical Summary

Modern Bulgaria was born in 1878, when five hundred years of Turkish occupation were brought to an end by a war between czarist Russia and the Ottoman Empire. This event, known to all Bulgarians as the Liberation, was followed by the establishment of a constitutional monarchy. In the wake of World War I, during which Bulgaria was allied with Germany and Austria-Hungary, national elections brought the Agrarian Party to power. Led by the charismatic Aleksander Stamboliyski, the Agrarians were initially supported by the Communist Party. However, in June 1923 Stamboliyski was assassinated and the government overthrown in a coup d'état. Though the Communists at first adopted a wait-and-see attitude, in September they sparked an insurrection, one that was drowned in blood and forced a number of Communist leaders to flee the country. For the next decade and a half, a series of authoritarian regimes governed the country. At the outbreak of World War II, Bulgaria was allied with Nazi Germany. However, the country neither took an active part in the war effort nor cooperated in the persecution of its native Jewish population. The Communist Party was declared illegal, which led to the creation of several resistance—or partisan—groups by 1941.

Bulgaria's postwar fate was decided at the Yalta Conference, which assigned the country to the Soviet zone of influence. This fate was sealed on 9 September 1944, when the Red Army entered and occupied Bulgaria. In the aftermath of this second "liberation," the Fatherland Front, which was the name given to the wartime antifascist coalition in Bulgaria, came to power. Though they were just one among a number of participating parties, the Communists held the critical posts of minister of the interior and minister of justice. Over the next few years, the other coalition parties knuckled under to the

Communist ascendancy; those who resisted were labeled "opposi-
tionists" and executed (as was most notably the case with Nikola
Petkov, the leader of the Independent Agrarian Party). Georgi Dimitrov, who was leader of the Communist Party, "hero" of the Reich-
stag fire trial in 1933, secretary general of the Komintern, and an
active participant in Stalin's purges after fleeing to the Soviet Union,
returned to Bulgaria in 1945 and became head of state. The first
trials against veteran Communists (echoing the prewar Stalinist
purges of the Russian Revolution), climaxing with the execution of
Traycho Kostov, took place in 1948–49. Upon Dimitrov's death in
1949, power soon passed to Vŭlko Chervenkov (1950–56), whose
policies were inspired by the Stalinist model. It was under Chervenkov that the farms were forcefully collectivized, the peasantry was
obliged to join cooperatives, and massive investments were made in
heavy industry. In 1956 Chervenkov was forced from power, and
his place was gradually assumed by Todor Zhivkov.

Bulgaria pursued an orthodox pro-Soviet policy under Zhivkov, but by the 1980s a new element was added: the persecution of
native Turks. Frightened by the growth of the Turkish minority, the
Bulgarian leadership ordered the Bulgarization of names, outlawed
the use of the Turkish language, and forbade Muslim religious practice. This policy of cultural repression sparked a massive exodus of
the persecuted minority into Turkey. On the eve of 1989, Zhivkov
sensed that the wind was changing direction, and he tried to present
himself as a reformer. But the effort failed, and he was deposed by
yet other Communist reformers in November 1989. Finally, in the
legislative elections of late 1991, the non-Communist opposition
won a majority of the seats and assumed the reins of government.

Let us now return to the days immediately after Bulgaria's
"liberation," which heralded the Communist repression. In September 1944 the partisans "avenged" themselves by summarily executing tens of thousands of victims. This hecatomb included active
fascists and members of the political police, but also many others
whose sole crime was to belong to the non-Communist intelli-
gentsia, professional or bourgeois classes. In fact, the crime could
extend to simply displeasing a Communist cadre. Dimitrov actively
encouraged these massacres: in a telegram sent from Moscow just

a week after the Red Army had arrived in Sofia, he called for the "torching of all signs of Bulgarian jingoism, nationalism, or anti-Communism." Following suit, the Central Committee, in a circular dated 20 September 1944, called for the liquidation of all the nests of "anti-Communist resistance" and the extermination of all "counterrevolutionaries."

In October 1944, the People's Tribunal was created, a special court devoted to the postwar purge. The death penalty was pronounced 12,000 times, and more than 2,700 individuals were ultimately executed. By way of comparison, between 1941 and 1944—the years of active Communist resistance—357 people were sentenced to death and actually executed (all crimes included). The political and social repression was given a juridical basis in early 1945. A government decree authorized the creation of the so-called Work Education Centers, known in Bulgarian as the TVO, or *Trudovo-vŭzpitatelni obshtezhitya*. TVO was a euphemism for concentration camp. All of the constituent parties of the Fatherland Front, including those who would soon be its victims, approved this decision. The profiles of those for whom the camps were created covered two major categories: in one were placed pimps, blackmailers, beggars, and idlers, while the second included all those individuals judged political threats to the stability and security of the state. The task of executing this decree was given to the Ministry of the Interior—more precisely, the omnipotent Office of State Security—rather than the Ministry of Justice. A series of laws and decrees enacted over the next ten years reaffirmed and sharpened the powers of the state police.

There were six major stages in the history of the concentration camps in Bulgaria.

(1) 1945 to 1949. There was forced labor at numerous work sites across Bulgaria. The camps were built in the vicinity of dams under construction, coal mines, and certain agricultural areas. Among the most notorious were Bobov Dol, Bogdanov Dol, Rositsa, Kutsian, Bosna, Nozharevo, and Chernevo.

(2) 1949 to 1953. Political prisoners were gathered from other camps and regrouped in the camp of Belene, located on Persin, a small island in the Danube and bordering on Romania.

(3) 1954 to 1956. Deportations to the camps were dramatically reduced, if not ended altogether. Belene nevertheless continued to operate.

(4) 1956 to 1959. Belene welcomed a number of new prisoners in the wake of the failed Hungarian revolt in the fall of 1956, as well as a crime wave in Sofia in the early months of 1958.

(5) 1959 to 1962. Following a hunger strike among the prisoners, Belene was closed down in 1959. Those prisoners who were not freed—according to certain documents, there were 166—were transferred to a new camp at Lovech, which bordered a rock quarry. Several thousand new prisoners eventually joined this first contingent. In September 1961, a hundred or so women prisoners were sent to a neighboring camp in Skravena. In November, the quality of camp life at Lovech was noticeably improved. In the following spring of 1962, the Political Bureau created a commission led by Boris Velchev to visit Lovech. As a result, the camp was shut down in April.

(6) 1962 to 1989. State repression had its high and low points during this period. A decision rendered by the Political Bureau in 1962 established that an individual, without trial in court, could be imprisoned and assigned to forced labor for up to five years. This repression was solely administrative, aimed at those accused of "social parasitism" or "loose morals," and often a response to information provided by "people's organizations" such as the neighborhood sections of the Fatherland Front. In the 1980s, numerous members of the Turkish minority in Bulgaria were also sent to Belene.

According to the statistics provided in 1990 by an inquiry commission created by the Communist Party, between 1944 and 1962 there were approximately one hundred concentration camps in a country of eight million individuals. Some 12,000 men and women passed through these camps between 1944 and 1953, and another 5,000 between 1956 and 1962. One witness affirms that in 1952 there were, in Belene alone, about 7,000 inmates. Yet another estimates that there were 186,000 prisoners during this entire period. For the moment, it is very difficult to know the precise numbers.

The camps were not the only means the government used to rid itself of pariahs during this same period. The government also used the administrative practice of deportation, which entailed forced residence in distant corners of the provinces. It is known, for example, that between 1948 and 1953 approximately 25,000 people were deported.

For the period of Lovech and Skravena (1959–62), which is the context for the majority of the following accounts, we can recreate an organizational chart of state repression as it pertains to these camps. (Though the principal political and bureaucratic actors are listed, the reader must keep in mind that this list is far from exhaustive.)

(1) At the head of the Party and state is Todor Zhivkov, who in turn is assisted by a succession of prime ministers, including Anton Yugov, who was a former interior minister.

(2) Under their orders are placed the Interior Ministry, run by Georgi Tsankov, with the assistance of Mincho Minchev, who was attorney general and whose signature was required for any and all internments.

(3) At the next tier we find Mircho Spasov, who was vice-minister of the interior and in charge of the concentration camps. Alongside him was Colonel Delcho Chakŭrov, director of the Office of Internment and Deportation.

(4) The camp at Lovech was run by Colonel Ivan Trichkov (1959–61), who had previously commanded Belene. He was succeeded by Major Petŭr Gogov (1961–62). The next in command was Major Tsviatko Goranov, who oversaw the work details, and Lieutenant Nikolas Gazdov, who was the camp's representative from the Bureau of State Security. All of these officers, moreover, had previously served in other concentration camps.

(5) The camp's commanding officers were assisted by a team of low-ranking officers, noncommissioned officers, adjutants, and brigade chiefs, these last recruited from the criminals assigned to the camp.

Finally, a few words need to be said about the camp at Lovech. The city of Lovech, which gave its name to the camp, is located in central Bulgaria, at the edge of the Balkan Mountains. An abandoned rock quarry outside the city became the site for the last and harshest of the Communist labor camps. Before 1959, the labor camps had been spread across Bulgaria. But most were closed following the fall of Chervenkov, and the inmates were transferred to Lovech. The camp was under the direct authority of the Ministry of the Interior rather than the regional authorities. Most Bulgarians did not know of the camp's existence, yet for those who went afoul of the state, Lovech had a sinister reputation: it was known to be a place that one might never leave alive.

THE
INMATES

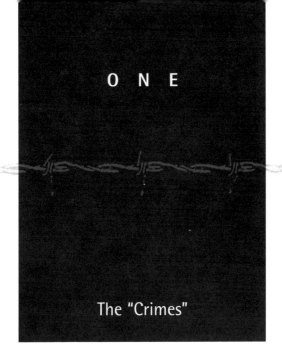

ONE

The "Crimes"

BORIS GIKOV

My father was a quiet and modest man who worked as a mason, while my mother kept house. To use a cliché that one finds even today in the police files, I come from a poor yet progressive family: my father was a member of the Communist Party, and my mother, whose brother belonged to one of the partisan groups, had helped them during the war.

I was born at the end of the 1930s, shortly before the start of the Second World War. As far as I can remember, the first years of my life were spent in basement apartments that reflected our poverty and misery. The small sum of money that my mother received upon her father's death was spent on an empty plot of land four miles outside of Sofia, on the road to Plovdiv. Nothing but fields stretched beyond our lot. With the help of my mother's family —she had a sister and six brothers, all of whom were masons—and my father's skill, we built our house. I grew up completely free in this distant neighborhood, far from the center of town. I was tall and well built as a boy, and always seemed older than my age. Until the very end of Vasil-Kolarov Junior High School, I was the tallest boy in my class.

At school and at play I had a great friend. Nasko—whose real name was Atanas Georgiev—and I were inseparable. We were happy-go-lucky kids, and we'd often meet others to dance in a small garden in front of the Church of the Seven Disciples. We spent most of our time there, dancing to the guitar music of other friends. This was in the summer of 1954, when I was just fifteen years old. There were also get-togethers held at the Teachers Union, the Alliance Française, and other places we frequented. At times there were confrontations with young kids from other neighborhoods, all for a girl's attention. Rumbles sometimes broke out, and eight of us, including Nasko and myself, were eventually hauled into court and charged with juvenile delinquency. We were hit with a year's imprisonment and sent to a correctional center for young men in Kazichane. This punishment was to have dire consequences.

After having served our sentence, I took evening courses at a local high school, while Nasko went to a vocational school. I then started to work as a machinist. I was young and strong and did a good job. Following this stint, I worked in a pharmaceutical factory ... in short, my days as a young troublemaker were over. In 1957 my mother died, leaving me and my father behind. My dad worked as a hospital watchman and moonlighted as a mason. It was at this same time that certain troubling events took place. In front of the passengers of a crowded tram car, a young man was killed by a sadistic character nicknamed "the Dog."

NIKOLAS DAFINOV

I was born in 1942. Unfortunately, though my family was "politically enlightened," it was not "actively engaged against the fascists."[1] My

---

1. This was an official distinction that opened the door to various privileges.

grandfather had studied pharmacy in the Austrian city of Graz. Two years after the liberation, he returned to Bulgaria and opened pharmacies in Tŭrnovo and Sukhindol. A decent man who was well liked by the townspeople, he would get up in the middle of the night to prepare medicine for sick children. He wouldn't accept money from his poorest clients, and was always ready to lend them a hand. After the events of 9 September,[2] he was labeled a "bourgeois," his pharmacies were expropriated, and he died in straitened circumstances. My grandmother was a schoolteacher who also did much charity work. My other grandfather was the prefect of Pleven under Stamboliyski;[3] identified as an Agrarian, he was harassed to the end of his life. As for my father, he went to Nancy (France) for dental studies.

I grew up in the years just after the Second World War, with its train of scarcity, ration tickets, and birth of the Communist regime. So it's not surprising that instead of receiving a scholarship to study abroad, I spent my time carrying coal up the stairs to our fourth-floor apartment and getting up at five o'clock in the morning in order to buy milk with the ration card for my baby sister. I studied at night, usually by candlelight.

I enjoyed foreign languages and was good at them. This was tantamount to treason at the time, since it implied interest in the West. I learned French at the Alliance Française. It was closed soon thereafter, and I was very eager to continue my studies at a bilingual school. I couldn't, however, since these schools had either been closed as well or were open only to those favored by the regime.[4] I could probably have gone to either the Suvorov or Nakhimov Naval Academies and become a naval officer, but once again I didn't have the correct political qualifications.[5] As a result, I studied

2. See the Historical Summary.
3. See the Historical Summary.
4. Schools where the curriculum is taught in a foreign language have always been sought after in Bulgaria. But the prewar schools were private and required tuitions, while under the Communists they were reserved for the regime's elite.
5. Elite military schools (the army or navy) were limited to young boys from politically safe families.

on my own and with the help of individual teachers. I learned
French, Italian, and English, and around 1957–58, I had a circle of
friends with similar interests. We talked and practiced among ourselves. My pursuits were not well received. After the regime eliminated opposition parties and imprisoned or deported thousands of
innocent men and women, they next targeted those citizens
attracted to the West, who listened to foreign music and talked politics. Once this group had been dealt with, it was the turn of those
who were simply indifferent to the regime and its activities.

In the search for guilty parties, we tend to focus upon the
upper echelons of the regime. We thus overlook the role played by
neighborhood organizations that depended upon the Fatherland
Front,[6] local housing officials, and other "conscientious" citizens
seeking to curry favor with the new regime. The opinion of the
Fatherland Front was sought on matters large and small. Since they
didn't always know the local population, the Front depended on
unverified information, giving free rein to their imagination. From
the Front, the information would pass on to the Ministry of the
Interior—or, more precisely, the Bureau of State Security. Those
who worked there were devoid of moral principles. Their one ambition was bureaucratic promotion.

But let me return to my own road to hell, one that I'd never
dreamed of even in my worst nightmares. In 1958–59, the first
foreigners began to cross the Iron Curtain. There were a few daring
businessmen, plus the occasional stray tourist, usually on his way
to Turkey. I'll never forget certain chance meetings with these
"enemies from the West." They were astonished to discover young
Bulgarians with whom they could talk and learn about life in our
country. This naturally led to the making of friendships, which were
as innocent as we were young, and which we didn't think to hide.
But this brought us to the attention of the "guardians of order."

One day I was out with a foreign family with whom I had
become friends. Blinded by my joy in practicing their language and
learning about the world on the other side of the Iron Curtain—

6. See the Historical Summary.

music, fashion, tourism—I fell into the hands of my greatest enemy. My new friends never knew what happened to that polite young Bulgarian who seemed so happy to chat with them. While these young "capitalists" waited for me to return from the restroom, I was approached by a man who introduced himself as a policeman. At first skeptical, I needed only a couple of minutes to believe him. He brought me to a room at 5 Moskovska Street, where two other men were waiting for us.[7] I couldn't get their names, and knew only that the name of the fellow who arrested me was Tzvetan Peshev (who has since died). The other two were like mad dogs and immediately pounced on me. Shouting threats and insults, they said they would beat me to death for being a bastard and an enemy of the state.

I managed to escape with a slap to the face and a promise to break off all contact with foreigners. When I got home, my legs were wobbly and my heart all in knots. I fell ill and stayed home for several days, not daring to tell others what had happened. It was only later that I learned that other friends who spoke foreign languages had similar experiences. One of them, Emil Pŭrvanov, worked as a bellboy at the Bulgaria Hotel. When I'd pass by the hotel to get him, we'd often fall into conversation with guests. Following a game between a visiting soccer team from Paris and a Bulgarian squad, we spoke to the French players. In a friendly gesture, they gave each of us a T-shirt and a few team badges. This provided the pretext for yet another arrest, and we were bundled off to the State Security offices. I had already made this trip to 5 Moskovska Street. This time, however, we were brought to a bigger office, filled with even more intimidating types. I recall the name Bakŭrdzhiev. The businesslike atmosphere in the office did not protect us from being punched and kicked. It was then that I was told, "You're going to be liquidated, you stupid bastard!" This phrase shocked me at the time, and I soon learned that they weren't joking around. We were let go after a few hours. Upset and in tears, Emil and I went home. We didn't know that the process of liquidation had already begun.

---

7. This is a street in downtown Sofia where the municipal office for the Ministry of the Interior was located.

BOZHIDAR PETROV

My father was one of the founders of Radio-Sofia. He was a director, scriptwriter, and actor. In 1962 Colonel Chakŭrov told him: "You managed to escape our Popular Tribunal, so now your sons will answer for your acts!"[8]

One day there was a ringing and pounding at the front door. The blows along with the curses grew louder. I leapt from my bed and ran straight into a group of police and plainclothesmen. Their pistols were drawn, and they shouted: "You've been listening to imperialist music! Who gave it to you? Where's your tape player? You're going to confess everything!"

My mother was crying, while my father tried to explain that I was a musician who played the violin, accordion, guitar. He told them that I liked authorized music. "Keep your explanations to yourself! We know which music is and isn't authorized!" They then grabbed the tape player and the only tape we had, and ordered my brother to throw his clothes on because he had some explaining to do at the police station. The tape player was never returned to us. Nor, at first, was my brother. He returned home about two years later. We heard that he had been taken to Belene. A letter arrived six months later. We petitioned and lodged legal complaints, but the courts told us that they had no file on my brother and that we should address the matter to the Ministry of the Interior. We wrote to the ministry, but never received an answer. My brother was nineteen years old at the time, and I was fourteen. It was 1957. After he finally returned home, he was drafted into the army. He was traumatized by his experiences, telling me about the beatings, the hunger, the hard labor.

Between the years 1959 and 1960 I was hauled into the Ministry of the Interior at 5 Moskovska Street seven times. They suspected me because I wore tight pants, listened to Western music, and danced to American songs. The first time followed a dance one

---

8. Chakŭrov was in charge of the Internment and Deportation Service in the Ministry of the Interior.

Saturday night at a club on Gocho Gopin Street. It was around eight o'clock when a large number of cops and plainclothesmen appeared and forced most of the boys to take off our pants while keeping on our shoes. Along with a few others, I refused to obey. We were pushed into a police van parked in front of the club and taken down to 5 Moskovska Street. We entered a waiting room, where our names were called out one by one. My turn came, and I was brought to a furnished room where two police officers were waiting. "Take off those pants, you little bastard," one of them shouted. He then walked up to me and struck me in the face.

"Wait! Why are you hitting me? I've done nothing!" I cried. "These pants are new, they're mine."

"Take him downstairs," the other officer ordered.

I was taken out of the room, and a guard led me down a flight of stairs that opens onto Dondukov Boulevard. To the left and across the street was a bar, while to the right was the door through which we were brought in. We continued down a series of spiral staircases that led to a big room that contained ten or so cell doors. One was opened, and I was pushed inside. The cell was small and completely empty. There was a lamp of sorts, but it barely cast any light. It was around ten o'clock. The silence was oppressive, broken only by the opening and closing of doors.

A good deal of time passed, and it must have been past midnight when I heard the pounding of boots on the concrete floor. Someone then shouted: "Off with your coats and jackets! Roll up your sleeves, remove your shoes and socks! Roll up your pants to your knees! Are you ready?"

I then heard the key turn in the lock. "Out!" a voice commanded. The others were also being ordered out of their cells. "Lie down, with your legs in the air." Screams filled the room. "Stop your crying, you son of a bitch! Count up to fifty." Something slammed.

"Tie the son of a bitch up!"

"Stick him on the chair."

More than an hour must have passed like that; then my turn came. They forced me to lie down near the door. Stretched out on

the floor, I lifted my legs as I was ordered to do. A plainclothesman stood over me, wearing a blue shirt with the sleeves rolled up
and a tie.

"You're going to count up to fifty out loud, and if you don't
scream too much you'll save your ass and be let go."

It started. Near me was another victim. A long rubber whip
whistled and came down on the soles of my feet. How could I
ever make you understand the pain? Trying not to cry too loud, I
counted up to fifty.

"Stand up!" My torturer was coated with sweat. "Hold out
your hands."

Sitting up, I started to get to my feet when a sharp pain
knocked me to my knees. I couldn't walk, and still on my knees, I
held out my hands.

"Count up to twenty," he ordered. He began to hit me while
I counted. The pain was bad, but it was nothing in comparison to
being whipped on the bottom of the feet.

"Now, go to the shower room. In one hour there will be an
inspection. Those of you who still have bruises will be beaten again."

I crawled on my stomach toward the showers.

Inside, there were about ten others stretched out on the
cement floor. My mouth was dry, and I needed water, but a mus-
tached thug wouldn't allow me to drink. My feet were so swollen
that they seemed to have been pumped with air. They had ballooned
grotesquely, and I could neither walk nor stand up. The cure, as it
turned out, was to wet the hands and rub the feet, then stamp up
and down till the swelling went down. Water ran out onto the
cement from a pipe. I wet my feet and pressed them against the
ground. The pain was overwhelming. Some of the others were
unable to stand long enough on their feet to go through the necessary acrobatics. We finished by running in place on the cement, then
in a circle around the large room, in the middle of which stood our
torturers. Pushing myself to the limit, I succeeded in getting my feet
"in order." I then underwent the "inspection." This meant showing
my hands, slapping them together several times, then lifting my feet
one after the other without lying down. If you passed the test, you

got dressed and put on your shoes. One of the torturers took me outside by the stairs. At the door he said: "Go home at once. If you tell anyone what happened here, we'll bring you back."

I went home and went to bed. It was four o'clock in the morning. I didn't say a word to my parents about what had happened, as I didn't want to worry them.

A few days later, I confided to a few friends what I had gone through. They advised me to lodge a legal complaint, but I didn't dare. And it was a good thing I didn't. About two months later, I saw those who did complain: they were back at 5 Moskovska Street, strapped to chairs in the basement. I say "later" because, despite my precaution, I myself was brought back to this place six more times. At the end of the second visit, all the torturers knew me and asked me to explain to the other unfortunate victims how to "cure" their swollen feet. Some of them were so shocked and scared that they didn't keep their legs in the air. Instead, they hit their heads against the ground, screaming and begging for mercy. This broke the torturers' rhythm. When this happened, the victim's legs were put on a chair and tied between the back and the seat. Or the victim was tied, sitting down in the chair, and was then pushed over onto the ground. He couldn't move in that position, and the blows against the feet were even more painful.

There were two kinds of whips: a thick one and a thin one. But I think one was as painful as the other. There were also sandbags the size of boxing mitts. Others were punched with them, mostly in the small of the back. I cannot say how much it hurt, though, since I was never hit with them. There were seven torturers. They were always dressed in civilian clothing—ties and rolled-up shirt sleeves—and they always stank of alcohol. They picked their victims and, when they grew tired of hitting us, would have a colleague take over. Three or four of them would hit us at the same time, but it was always different, though I do not know why. I knew victims who had complained; I knew others who stayed in the basement for months because their feet could not recover; I saw corpses. When a victim couldn't reduce the swelling of his feet, the torturers stopped beating him, because he could no longer feel the pain.

One day they were beating two brothers. One of them, no longer able to stand it, shouted, "Stop! He's small. Hit me instead!" His request was met, and they started to concentrate on him. He suddenly cried, "Wait! I've a father who's like you."

There was a moment of silence, followed by a barrage of questions concerning the identity and profession of the victim's father. "He's a doctor who works at the local slaughterhouse."

With that, they jumped him, shouting, "And so, you're saying we're butchers, you little bastard?" The whips cracked, and the older brother was badly beaten, but the younger one was left alone. Christo and Ivan were the names of the two boys.

In 1960, the torturers grew bolder. They began to hit us all over the body. On the chest, on the back. They were like mad dogs. They no longer bothered maintaining a cover of secrecy and no longer cared about "curing" the victims. The majority of these people are now retired. I meet them in the street, and they smile at me as if we were once good friends. They were "recycled" over the last thirty years and were placed in important positions controlled by the Ministry of the Interior. Georgi Pavlov was a colonel who commanded the police in Sofia. Rangelov was a colonel too, as was Bakŭrdzhiev, who was an advisor in the Interior Ministry. Georgiev was a colonel at Interior. I cannot remember the names of the three other torturers. But they were all Party members, were former partisans, and held important posts. They tortured me because I listened to Western music, wore tight pants, enjoyed American dancing, and because my father was a well-known figure in the world of culture before the Communist takeover.

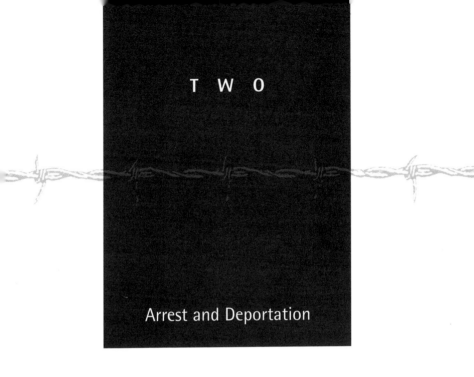

T W O

Arrest and Deportation

BORIS GIKOV

About 5:30 one morning in June 1959, there was a pounding at our door. Two plainclothesmen and a policeman then rushed into the house and carried out a search. They said they were looking for hidden arms. They found nothing and even signed a report to this effect. But they took me back to the station for a "small matter" of an identity check. I was taken to the police station at 1 Polyanov Street and locked in a basement prison cell. Nasko turned up a short time later, also brought in for a "small identity check." After a sleepless night, the two of us were loaded into a green truck and brought to the guardhouse at the central train station, where we were thrown into a cell with others who had been arrested.

The oldest among us asked why we'd been arrested and where

we were being sent. But no one knew. The next day we were hand-cuffed and loaded into a cattle car. At one of the train stops, someone looked through a small crack in the siding and recognized the station at Pleven. But it was only after the train passengers got off and left the station that our wagon doors were opened. We were hustled into rows of three and, with guards waving machine guns all about, were led to the station's guardhouse. The building was dilapidated and grim. Once inside, our handcuffs were removed, and we were locked in cells furnished with rotting wood beds. An old man in a striped uniform who had also been arrested told us that we were bound for the Belene concentration camp. According to him, thousands of men were locked away at Belene, where they were worked to death. They were worked until they met daily production quotas that could never be met; they worked regardless of how much time it took.

We passed yet another sleepless night.

At dawn, we were told to prepare our bags. Nasko and I each had a piece of stale bread and jam brought from Sofia. The same guards put on our handcuffs, and we got into the same cattle car, which took us to the station at Levski. We changed trains, getting into one marked "Levski-Belene." It was now clear that the old pris-oner was telling us the truth.

We reached Belene at ten o'clock in the morning and walked from the station to a bridge. We halted near some buildings, where officers were waiting. The guards gave them our official papers. After waiting there for two hours, we were taken across the bridge and to an island. We then picked up the pace until we reached the entrance to the camp, which was ten kilometers away. We could see barracks from the gates, but not a living soul.

We were put through a very careful body search upon our arrival. We were stripped naked, our heads were shaved, and in place of our own clothing we were given old army and prison fatigues. All of our personal effects were confiscated; I never saw them again. They then divided us into work brigades. Nasko and I were in the same brigade and in the same barracks. This was our only consolation in our grim situation.

When I say "barracks," something like sheds might come to

mind. But, in reality, they were underground shelters. Upon entering, you had to climb down a couple of steps in order to reach the room itself. It was divided by a corridor, and along each side were bunk beds with shredded, rotting mats covered by fraying military blankets. About a hundred people, piled on top of one another, lived in this room. The shelter itself was built with a mixture of cob and woven branches—the same material used for animal pens. Hygiene was out of the question, since the walls were alive with thousands of bedbugs, which never left us in peace and never allowed us to sleep. The mosquitoes were nearly as bad.

To occupy our time until the return of the work brigades, we carried wood until dusk. Since we weren't yet enrolled in the camp, we ate what we had brought along with us.

The camp directors were all officers: Colonel Trichkov, Major Gogov, Captain Atanasov, Major Neshev (his wife Totka Nesheva was in command of the female prisoners), Major Goranov, and yet others whose names I forget.

I learned from veteran prisoners about the trip to Work Site No. 2 the year before. The inmates, I was told, were herded by horse-mounted guards and wolfhounds trained for this very task. Cudgel blows rained down on the defenseless victims under the pretext that they were tramping across a plantation of young poplar trees. The fact of the matter is that there was neither a plantation nor poplars. The prisoners were so panicked, and tried so hard to avoid the club blows, that they didn't stop to pick up the possessions or clothing they had dropped.

The camp was surrounded by barbed-wire fences, more than two meters high, held fast by fence posts in the shape of an upside down *L*, like those in the fascist camps we saw at the movie theater. Along the fence every forty or fifty meters were wooden towers. They were manned by armed watchmen with orders to fire immediately on anyone who passed beyond the warning signs on the perimeter.

Everything at the camp was done to bugle blasts. Going to bed, getting up, breakfast, lunch, roll call. The roll call took place after dinner; one could never predict how long it would last. We stood along three sides of a rectangle while a guard called out, brigade by brigade, the prisoners' first and last names. It was as if we were in prison. The length of the roll calls seemed that much longer during the cold winter nights.

In the middle of the summer the barracks were oppressive, all the more so because we were packed in like sardines. I spent that first night waiting for the bugle call at five o'clock without ever closing my eyes. Once it sounded, absolute pandemonium broke out. A hundred prisoners were trying to dress and walk at the same time. They pushed one another while rushing toward the sinks and toilets in order to be the first ones there.

At our work site alone, there must have been two or three thousand prisoners. There were, among us, political prisoners, common-law criminals, convicts, and still others. It was impossible to make sense of this jumble of people, and Nasko and I did our best to stick together. We were sent to the Eleventh Work Brigade, which turned out to be a punitive measure. Nearly all newcomers had to pass through this gauntlet.

We went to our site, accompanied by machine-gun-carrying guards and a brigade chief, who, like us, was an inmate. We were then divided into groups of two and given our daily production quota. We had to dig, load, and transport ten cubic meters of sand and dirt in wheelbarrows. The women prisoners, it seems, had a norm of eight cubic meters.

Unless you've tried, you cannot know how hard it is to push wheelbarrows full of sand. Part of the load inevitably falls out with each step. Those who couldn't fill the quota—which happened to Nasko and I several times—were recalled after dinner and had either to cut wood or to load the food silos for the camp livestock till late into the night. The veteran prisoners called this work detail "dance night," since we worked under the blaze of search lights.

Although the work schedule was intense, we managed to find enough food to stave off death. We were allowed to receive one hundred leva every three months along with a package of five kilos.[1]

1. This is based on the Bulgarian currency during this period. At that time, a monthly salary was from 2,000 to 3,000 leva. A "new lev" later replaced ten old leva.

However, the delivery of the packages depended on the whim of the officers, who rewarded model prisoners. In five months, I received just one package. We were also allowed to send letters every three months. The letters were censored, and we weren't allowed to describe our lives in detail. About all we could write was "All is well."

So much for our rewards. As for the punishments, they were horrible. Those of us sentenced to solitary confinement were sent to a sort of dungeon with several cells. Each one was about a square meter in size. Those locked inside were forced to remain standing in water up to their ankles.

We worked for about a month on a dike, and then Nasko and I were assigned to a fishing brigade made up of sixteen men and two flat-bottomed boats. We caught the fish in a huge net with which we would block out part of the marsh. We tossed into the boat whatever we caught. We spent nearly a month on the boats, and were able to supplement our diets with fish.

A group of us, including Nasko and I, were then transferred to Work Site No. 1, which was a kilometer away from No. 2. We were divided into groups to work outdoors. About forty of us were sent to the village of Alexandrovo in order to join a project on the Osŭm River. We were housed in a barracks located on a small island in the middle of the river. Though we were still guarded, the atmosphere was more relaxed. After twenty or so days a torrential downpour struck, lasting three entire days and nights. When we awoke on the fourth day, water was up to our knees in the barracks. The bridge that connected us to the mainland had been swept away by the waters; not a trace of it was to be seen. We were ordered to find and reassemble the construction material. Naked down to our belts, we gathered and dragged ashore wood planks that had been caught in the branches of willow trees. The water had turned terribly cold in the downpour, and we had to change our clothing every thirty minutes. By nightfall we had succeeded in rebuilding the bridge. This happened in early September 1959.

It was then that our group was ordered to return to Belene. It seems that instructions had been given to close the camp, which existed under the heading of "Section 0789." All the prisoners were assembled at Work Site No. 1 and told that the camp would be closed. Immediately afterward, large numbers of prisoners were released. All of us thought that we'd soon be seeing our loved ones again.

While the camp was breaking up, names were called from a list. Since identification papers weren't required, Nasko answered to someone else's name and was freed. On the other hand, I ignored Nasko's prodding and waited for my own name to be called. I've long since regretted my honesty.

Following the departure of the liberated prisoners on 3 September 1959, there only remained about 140 people in the camp. We were told that we would stay to help with the harvest and that our own liberation was imminent. We waited through all of September. Finally, we would wait no longer and went on a hunger strike.

Very early one morning in the middle of October, we were loaded onto trucks covered with canvas and left for an unknown destination. I don't remember how long the journey lasted, but we eventually noticed that we had passed through Lovech. Three kilometers or so from Troyan, we turned off the road, to the right, and entered a tunnel that led under a train track. We came to a halt at the foot of a tree-covered hill.

As we were getting out of the truck, I noticed that the guards and officers waiting for us were the same ones from our earlier camp—but even more bloody-minded and furious. "We're going to die here," I said to myself.

NIKOLAS DAFINOV

In December 1960, I fell ill for a few days and was unable to go to school. On the tenth, at five o'clock in the morning, the doorbell began to ring furiously, while someone started kicking at the door. My entire family panicked. My father opened the door, and I heard my name uttered in the hallway. Three uniformed men were insisting that I go with them for questioning to Police Station No. 6. They offered no other information. Through her sobs, my mother was asking why I had to be taken away. Suddenly, the policemen burst into my room and tore me from bed. I was forced to dress quickly, and thinking I'd soon be back home, I put on the first things within reach. A jeep was waiting outside, and I was taken to the station. I was thrown into a jail cell, where I was completely ignored for two hours. I was then taken out and, without the least word of explanation, brought to the guardhouse at the train station. There were about thirty others already locked up there, and they immediately began to ask me questions. I was shocked: they asked me how many years I was in for, which prison I had been sentenced to, and so forth. I explained that I hadn't been convicted of anything, but most of them thought I was lying.

Early the next morning, I was handcuffed with two other prisoners and taken on board the Sofia-Varna train. Two enormous guards kept on our handcuffs till we reached the guardhouse at Mezdra. There I met yet other cellmates, who, like the others, refused to believe that I hadn't been convicted of a crime and that I'd no idea where I was being sent. The next day I was again in transit, this time to Pleven. As destiny would have it, I found myself in the company of brighter companions in that rancid-smelling guardhouse. I learned that they were political prisoners. I was depressed by the fact that I didn't know where I was going. Adding this to my fatigue from two solid days of sleepless travel left me a less than ideal conversationalist. Soon thereafter, an impressively tall man brought into our cell announced that he was from Belene. There followed the usual questions and my negative answers, which had grown so disagreeable for me. The tall fellow looked at me with concern and said, "My boy, let's at least hope that you won't be sent to Lovech. Though there isn't a single convict there, it's as if everyone has been sentenced to death!"

The blood rushed to my head. I heard his words as if in a dream. At Belene there had been talk of a "death camp." Those sent there never returned!

I tried to steady myself and to reflect as clearly as possible on my situation. I couldn't believe that my experiences at 5 Moskovska

Street would condemn me to die so young. But the words of my last torturer ("We're going to liquidate you, you little bastard!") continued to haunt me.

The man who shared this awful information with me said that he would be freed in a few months. I asked him if he would be visiting Sofia, and he replied that he often had the occasion to do so. I wanted to find some way to let my mother know what had become of me. I took off my gold cross that I'd worn around my neck since my baptism, and asked the man if he would return it to my family, telling them what he had seen and the fate that was in store for me. At that very moment, I was certain that I was going to my death. He took the cross and put it on his own chain, promising to carry out my wish. As it turned out, my mother never received the cross. But God nevertheless saved my life by giving me the strength to survive. I now realize this was a gift.

The next morning, I was once again taken to a train, which was headed to Varna. I was still disturbed from what I had heard the day before, and when I was taken off the train at Levski and placed on one for Lovech, the words of my torturer at Moskovska Street became all too real.

BOZHIDAR PETROV

The last time I was beaten up was in 1960, but as I already said, all the officials knew me, just as I knew who they were. They arrested me in the street along with two friends of mine, Gocho and Ioncho. No reason was given; they had simply caught sight of me. As for my friends, they were arrested because they were with me. The police car was parked nearby, and we were pushed inside. Before you knew it, we were back in the basement at 5 Moskovska Street. They beat up Ioncho and then let him go. A few years later, he fled Bulgaria and now lives in Sweden. They then started in on Gocho, who shouted, "Stop! My father works in the Ministry of the Interior." They asked him lots of questions, and one of the torturers momentarily left the dungeon. It turned out that Gocho wasn't lying: his father had been a "freedom fighter against fascism" and worked at

Interior. His father then appeared in the dungeon, and Gocho ran into his arms. He said he was innocent of any crime and had been arrested without reason. He also asked his father to have me freed. His father knew me, but he only had his son released. Gocho got off lightly: twenty backlashes. He eventually escaped to the United States, where he now lives.

I was hit twenty times on the hands, then twenty times on the soles of my feet. This time, however, I wasn't let go after the beating. Instead, I was taken to a car and driven to Police Station No. 1. I spent New Year's Day 1961 there. I was kept twenty days and was never told why I'd been arrested. But it's also true that I never asked, since I wasn't keen on seeing my torturers again. I also celebrated my eighteenth birthday at the police station. Apparently, this was the reason why I was kept in detention for twenty days.

Sometime between 10 and 12 January 1961, I was bundled into a car and taken to the guardhouse at the train station in Sofia. I spent the night there, and the next morning I was handcuffed and loaded onto a train. I wasn't told where I was being sent. The policemen guarding me rotated constantly. A few of them seemed to pity me. In fact, one policeman removed my handcuffs, said that I wasn't dressed warmly enough and that I should have been allowed to take heavier clothing. This went on for three days, until three more prisoners were taken on board, I believe, at Levski. They were all between forty and fifty years old. We barely exchanged two words. They were terribly frightened and said, "Ah, my boy, if you knew where we're headed. May you make it out alive." I listened to them and thought back to 5 Moskovska Street. Where could they be taking me while my feet weren't yet healed?

A covered truck was waiting for us at Lovech. The trip lasted about an hour.

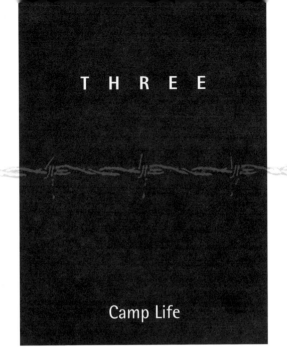

T H R E E

Camp Life

NIKOLAS DAFINOV

Two guards were waiting for me at the train station in Lovech, and they led me across town on foot. We walked for half an hour, eventually left the town limits and found ourselves in the gorge running along the Osŭm River. Suddenly, on my right appeared watchtowers manned by policemen armed with machine guns. Five minutes later, we walked through a tunnel—I heard a train pass above us—and some fifty meters further came to a hill. We passed some squat buildings, and the guards left me in front of one. To the left, there was an encampment surrounded by barbed wire, a second gate, and, once again, watchtowers at each corner.

The door to the building opened, and a tall savage-looking fellow appeared at the doorway. His face was repulsive: his teeth were spaced like a wild boar and his hair resembled a brush. The guards gave him an envelope sealed with red wax and left. I remained on the threshold, while this monstrous apparition read the papers just given to him. When he was done, he reached for a stick with a hooked end that was on his desk. Why the cane? I wondered. I hadn't noticed that he limped. He turned toward me and said that I was surprisingly young to be such a bastard. He then began to strike me with the stick. His words were punctuated by terrible blows across my entire body. I was stunned and began to scream from sheer fear and pain, but my cries were smothered, and all I heard was "Bastard, bastard." I fell to the ground, and covering my head with my hands, I missed the arrival of a second man. I glanced quickly in his direction and saw something resembling Quasimodo, also carrying a stick. As it turned out, I wasn't far wrong: this apparition was not human. He was clubfooted, his body was twisted, his face was horrible and blackened, and a cigarette was wedged in a toothless mouth. "Take him away, Shakho!" the other fellow shouted. These men were Gazdov[1] and Shakho the Gypsy. Quasimodo shouted at me, "Get to the door, fast!"

Blows from his stick rained down on my back. I hurried ahead in order to escape, but was ordered to stop. I obeyed, and when Shakho reached me, he began to pound me again with his stick. He knocked me to the ground and called me a "maraud," short for "marauder." I knew that this old word meant someone who stole, especially during wartime. But why was I being called a "thief"?

We stopped in front of a sagging barracks, from which a man stepped out. He wore thick glasses and seemed to be a relatively decent sort. He waved Shakho away and said that he'd give me warmer clothing. While he was rummaging through a pile of filthy clothes, he asked me if I'd been badly beaten. When I nodded yes, he began to explain the camp "rules." Only then did I realize that the man who first "welcomed" me was a ranking camp officer.

The fellow wearing the glasses was named Willy Tadger. He treated me well and told me that my welcome could have been much

---

1. Gazdov was the camp's police chief. See his account on pages 147–52.

worse. Some prisoners were beaten to death upon their arrival. Along with Shakho and Gazdov, all the camp guards, including those prisoners placed in charge of the brigades, carried sticks. When I asked Tadger if it was true that everybody died here, his sad eyes looked at me through the thick square lens: "Yes, it is. But let's hope that God protects us."

When he finally found his stock of "best clothing," I was shocked. The overcoat was sleeveless, the pants were torn below the knees, the jacket was in shreds ... but worst of all were the shoes, which were riddled with big holes. Willy nevertheless did his best: he gave me rags I could turn into socks. I couldn't help wondering what else I was going to discover here.

Once decked out in my new gear, I gazed at my surroundings. I couldn't really imagine what I must have looked like, and I was probably lucky that I didn't see Gazdov arrive at that same moment. He carried a pocket mirror so that inmates could see themselves for the "last time."[2] Once my head was shaved, I looked just like my fellow victims, who had by then started to appear from God knows where. One glance sufficed to show that they had not been out for a stroll. It was Sunday, and the prisoners had quit work at noon. Sunday afternoons were the only chance that prisoners had to relax and look after their personal affairs—or at least to the degree that such activity was possible. Three barrels were placed on the esplanade, and these miserable exhausted men lined up in three rows, having pulled out twisted mess tins from beneath their rags, into which three brigade leaders ladled out a mysterious liquid. I quickly got to know this unusual, unvarying dish: beans boiled in water with onions, rice, cabbage, and noodles.

Most of the prisoners ate standing up, while a few of the oldest rolled up their rags and sat on the ground. They seemed constantly on the lookout, glancing over their shoulders while they gulped down their vile brew. Lunch lasted just a few minutes. Once

2. Translator's note: As this account subsequently reveals, at morning roll call Gazdov would select certain prisoners, to whom he'd show the mirror with the command to look at themselves one last time. The same day, they would be murdered at the stone quarry.

it was over, the prisoners took note of my presence by repeating among themselves, "A new arrival, a new arrival." They looked at me with a mixture of pity and fear. Their expression was like that of a dog: not a dangerous dog, but one that's been starved and beaten.

All of the sudden, a man leapt toward me with a stick in his hands and shouted, "You, go get those barrels! Start washing them!" With that, he started to pound my back with the stick. Already dazed from the earlier beatings, I could barely stand. My entire body burned. I washed the barrels in a large basin lined with five faucets, from which ice-cold water poured. This area doubled as our bathroom. Anyone who has never felt water immediately turn to ice on one's hands can never imagine what I endured that December day. Since I was a newcomer, I was quickly surrounded by several people. They asked me where I came from and what I had done to deserve this fate. Without exception they made it clear that I'd been sentenced to a world from which one didn't return. Willy soon appeared and told me that I could write a letter to my parents to tell them where I was. Whether the camp officers would mail it was another story. Willy advised me not to complain or say too much. In fact, for my parents' sake, it would be best to write—if I could find the strength to do so—something lighthearted. The officers read everything, and they decided if the letters could be mailed.

Willy Tadger was also a prisoner. He was known as the "camp brain." The officers employed him as secretary and scribe, and for any other task that their primitive educations prevented them from doing. He told me how the camp was created. It all started when about one hundred prisoners who went on a hunger strike at Belene were brought here as punishment. It was near the end of 1959. They built the barracks themselves, then were put to work in the two stone quarries near the camp. The camp's first commandant was Colonel Trichkov, who had been in charge of Belene. He retired in 1960 and was replaced by Major Gogov. Gogov was a small cruel man who, like Trichkov, used his stick freely. Lieutenant Gazdov worked for the Bureau of State Security, whose monstrous actions were feared by one and all.

I pointed to about a dozen prisoners armed with sticks and

asked who they were. Willy replied that they were prisoners like us whom we had to obey because they had been chosen as brigade leaders. An old political prisoner whispered to me, "They're very dangerous! All of them have black pasts and have spent time in jail. They're all alike and were deliberately chosen by the camp officers."

While we were speaking, two or three of these men came up to me. "Hey you, the new recruit!" they barked. "This isn't going to be a party. Are you an egghead like your pal over here? We don't like your sort around here."

Willy took me to the barracks where I'd be sleeping, and stepping inside, I nearly fainted. It was beyond anything I'd ever imagined about prisons and the limits of misery. It was like a stable. Along the wall stretched wooden bunk beds that had been nailed together. On top were shredded straw mattresses covered with army blankets. I was told that after evening roll call—which I'll describe in more detail—the barracks doors were locked. The one hundred men trapped inside had to make do with a single lamp and a pail to relieve themselves.

I said that I nearly fainted inside the barracks, but it wasn't really the sight of the interior that was responsible. There were only about ten or fifteen people inside, lying down and groaning. What overwhelmed me was an awful odor that permeated the room and took me by the throat. I felt as if I were suffocating.

I quickly walked out and continued to speak with Willy. He was, as I've already mentioned, a cultivated man. I felt even closer to him when I discovered that he spoke French. He explained what rights we theoretically had as prisoners, though in reality we had none. The only thing I could hope for was that my first letter would reach my family. I was to write my first and last name on the envelope, along with the fateful address: Section 0789, Ministry of the Interior, Lovech, Stone Quarries.[3] I also was told to be very careful

3. Nicolas Dafinov's parents saved the first letter they received from their son. It reads:

11/12/60, Camp Lovech.

Dear Mama, Papa, and Lidi,

when I addressed one of the brigade chiefs. We were required to say "Citizen Warden," as though we were in prison. But as Willy "reassured" me, our lot was a thousand times worse than that of ordinary prisoners.

No one bothered me until the evening roll call, perhaps because I was with Willy. At a certain point, the bugle sounded and a warden appeared on the esplanade. It must have been about 7:30. The wretched prisoners ran and quickly lined up, occupying three sides of the rectangle. I managed to find my place in a row. In front of each group stood a man who counted the inmates and reported to the warden. They were all armed with clubs. While the roll call was going on, two men armed with clubs appeared in front of our group. One was dressed in civilian clothing, while the other wore a major's uniform. The civilian was the terrifying man who had first welcomed me to the camp, while I was told that the other was Goranov.

They began to pull men from the row, one after the other, and brutally hit them. The blows were accompanied by humiliations, insults, and all sorts of filth. They hit those who hadn't met the

---

I must tell you what has happened: I am at a Work Reeducation Camp in Lovech. As I write to you my eyes are full of tears because if I'd listened to a tenth of what you told me, I don't believe I'd now be here. Dear Mama, the one thing I ask of you is not to worry and try to relax. I know it's very hard for you but I believe that one day you'll see the son you deserve. Life is hard and we do not stop learning. I beg you from the depths of my heart to forgive me for all the pain I have caused you.

The day I return you will see a completely changed son.

I've the right to receive and send a letter every three months, 100 leva each month, and 15 kilograms of food every three months. One can also send a 5-kilogram package of food every month.

Please send me a cotton quilt, a couple of pairs of socks, an old fur vest, and cheap rubber boots, size 43. Send them in a separate package, clearly marking "Clothes" on the box, since I don't want to lose the right to receive a food package. My address is:

Nicolas Dafinov, Section 0789, Ministry of the Interior, Lovech, Stone Quarries.

I am in good health for now, and will use every ounce of my strength to become a truly worthy man. I hug you with all my heart and send you a thousand kisses. Stay well, kisses to Papa and Lidi, and ask you all to be brave. I'll wait for my one joy: your letter. Your son, Nicolas.

quota,[4] those who had collapsed from the heavy labor, those whom they simply didn't like, and yet others for no reason at all. The beaten men were then sent flying back to their rows by a kick. Once there, the brigade chiefs would take over the bloody work, beating them yet again.

How could I ever describe the terror I felt when I heard my name called out? My neighbors pushed me, urging me to step forward. I must have been dragging my feet, since Shakho, the one who looked like Quasimodo, struck me a couple of times in the back. When I made it to the middle of the esplanade and stood between the two officers, Gazdov rested his club on my shoulder and growled: "You understand that you're here to work? Work and do nothing else but work? You're no longer in the world out there, where you can loaf about. Starting tomorrow, you'll work with the thieves."

He clubbed me a few times on the shoulder. I screamed out in pain, but he shouted twice as loud as I did: "Get back in line, bastard!"

4. Many of the prisoners recall being punished for not meeting the quota. One of them describes how this rite unfolded:

We worked in teams at the quarry, each team having five men. We worked, but if the quota wasn't met, blows would follow. We were beaten during the day, and it happened that two members of our team were killed, and so only three of us were left. Try as we might, we couldn't fill the quota. At roll call that night, we arranged ourselves in rows. In the middle of the rectangle there was a lot of dust. Gazdov drew a circle of sorts in the dirt with his stick and ordered the fifth team to step forward. We did so. "Why didn't you fill the quota?" "But citizen major, two team members died." (We didn't have the right to say that they had been killed.) "Step into the circle." I did so, and he started to beat me with his stick. I tried to protect myself, of course, but he kept hitting me, hitting me, hitting me. When he stopped, he kicked me in the ribs. I was ready for the sack. Yes, I was. But at the time we were young and solid. Christo [a friend] ran to me, and I remember nothing else. He took me in his arms, even though he had been beaten as well, and took me to a room. That is how I survived. Even though it was a real pigsty, with excrement everywhere. He left me there. The next day I was back on my feet and had escaped the sack and went back to work. (*The Survivors*)

It wasn't over. When I got back in line, the clubfooted monster welcomed me with his stick. My arm was completely numb. I was overcome by panic. If this were to continue another day or two. . . . I already saw myself liquidated, as they'd promised I'd be back in Sofia. I was too stunned to see or hear what was happening on the esplanade. But, suddenly, everyone began to run to the barracks' door. In a couple of seconds, everyone was inside; some were already in bed. Nobody undressed; they took off only their shoes and used them as pillows. I did the same, and settled down in the forty centimeters of bed that I shared with a neighbor. Nobody spoke. Each of us tried to find the most comfortable position to sleep. I was bruised all over, but it wasn't that that kept me from falling asleep. The pervasive smell, heavy and sticky, that I had smelled when I first entered the room gripped me again by the throat. I turned around in my bed, waking up my neighbor. He turned toward me and spoke. We introduced ourselves to one another, and I finally asked the question that had been tormenting me. The smell. . . . My neighbor looked sadly at me, patted me on my swollen shoulder and said, "It's the pus running from wounds, my boy. That's the awful smell. Worms get into some of the wounds, but those are cleaned in the infirmary."

Perhaps he would have gone on talking, but he was overpowered by sleep. But when I also closed my eyes, I thought I saw worms crawling in front of me. I tried to imagine Sofia, my home, my loved ones. I began to cry softly and fell into semiconsciousness. I don't remember what I dreamed this first nightmarish night, but certainly not of green fields. This was how my new life began—a life devoted to my reeducation.

Toward five o'clock in the morning, I snapped awake to screams and inhuman moans. We were being sent off to work with cudgel blows, but we first had to perform our morning "ablutions." There weren't many people in front of the sinks, but there was a long line waiting in front of the few holes serving as toilets.

Most of the men were already lined up on the esplanade, in

front of the stable where we slept, waiting for the arrival of the tureens filled with our breakfast. Willy brought me a bowl from the storeroom as well as a torn bag. I got in line for my tea and a microscopic portion of jam.

Once again there was the roll call taken by the two adjutants armed with clubs. And then we left for work. Since the evening before I had known that I was going to work with the "marauds," the sick prisoners who had been savagely beaten. Shakho was the brigade chief. We lined up in rows of four, each of us holding the arm of the next in line. With that, the column of foul-smelling beggars, covered with pus-filled wounds, left the barbed-wire confines of the camp. We were accompanied by ten or so uniformed guards pointing their machine guns at us, along with another ten or so men carrying clubs. They occupied themselves on the way to the quarry by beating the unlucky ones who stumbled and fell behind the column.

It was 5:30 A.M., 19 December. Searchlights lit our interminable walk to the "quarry of death." I was seventeen years old, and I couldn't understand what I'd suddenly become. I understood even less why all of this had happened. I was walking toward the rear of the group. Behind us two prisoners were pushing a handcart that reminded me of a stretcher. It was to carry back those who died. This, too, I learned on 19 December 1960. The convoy made its way along the muddy path on this somber winter morning. About a kilometer down the road, barbed wire rose up and the group came to a stop. Some of us stayed at this spot, which lodged a stone crusher and was called the "silo." The quarry was very deep and lined with dozens of galleries. In my opinion, between fifty and sixty people worked there, three to a gallery, while the others pushed the wagons and helped crush the stone. Two of the club-carrying men stayed at the crusher: Blagoy Gaytanski[5] (known as the Donkey) from Plovdiv, and Konstantin Peshev from Stanke Dimitrov. Part of the armed guard and two wardens wielding sticks also stayed. The rest of the convoy began to climb down a steep path. We kept slipping in the frozen mud, but held on to one another's arms. Once past

5. See his account on pages 139–40.

this obstacle, we saw stretching out in front of us the "quarry of death." Searchlights were trained on it from all sides. Compared to the "silo," this quarry was shallower, but three times as big. There were many more galleries, and a large ramp led right up to the rail tracks for the Lovech-Troyan line. There were watchtowers on every side.

———

When I first started at the quarry, fewer people were there than in the months that followed, when some four to five hundred worked in the pits. At the front of each gallery, there were five or six people with hammers and levers, rakes and shovels. One was in charge of the cart. Once loaded with stones, the carts were pushed up the ramp, where the train had to be loaded in ten or fifteen minutes. There were about thirty train cars, and each handcart carried about 750 centimeters of rock. At first, the quota for five men was thirty carts. It was raised to fifty, and finally to seventy-five carts. It was around six o'clock when the prisoners quickly took their positions and went to work. In my gallery, the majority of people had been horribly beaten the night before, and painfully set about their tasks. Those even worse off—and there were many—remained below. They used smaller hammers than ours, and broke stones that had already fallen to the ground. They were unable to stand on their feet and had to work while kneeling down. This didn't escape the attention of the guards, and each time they passed in front of this pile of human flesh, they lashed out with their clubs. These poor fellows rarely returned to camp on their feet. And when you weren't on your feet, that meant you were destined for the stretcher.

Since I was new and young, I was assigned to the cart. I filled it, then pushed it some twenty or thirty meters along the ramp. The winter was brutal, and the temperature was below zero Celsius. The pain from the blows I received the night before gripped my entire body. I did all I could to ignore it. I pushed a few carts down the ramp, and once they were emptied, I pushed them back to the gallery. The skin on my hands begin to stick to the frozen metal, but I could hardly expect pity from the guards. I saw the brigade leader,

Andrey, and one of the guards, Yozo the Valaque, beating some of my poor companions. They were guilty of having fallen short of their quota. Upon seeing me, they began to rub their hands in anticipation, especially Andrey. They called me a lazy little jerk and began to pummel me. Doubled over in pain, I fell to the ground near the cart. That made them even angrier. Hitting me with their clubs, they forced me to my feet and back to work. Having finished with us, they continued on to the next gallery. To avoid a repetition of this bloody experience, we got up and painfully went about our work.

At a certain point, I noticed a body lying on the ground. I walked up to him and saw that he was barely breathing. It was an old likable Jewish man from Sofia. He had had a commercial office in the building where the Crystal Café is now located. I can no longer recall his name, and to tell the truth, we barely got to know one another in the camp. He was also a new arrival, and had been there just a few days. I pulled him off to one side, propped up his head, and then hurried to push along another cart of rocks, since the slightest of delays meant the stick. When I got to the ramp, the cart had picked up so much speed that I lost control. The cart got jammed, and my hands were so painful that I could not push it back all alone. Old Zlatko, a lawyer from Sofia whose job was to count the number of carts, ran over to help me. A Gypsy dropped his pick axe and also came over to help. Working together, we succeeded in turning it around, pushing it up the ramp, and unloading it. I steered the cart back toward the gallery and felt tears running down my face due to the physical pain. It's only then that I saw the Jew, still lying on the ground, but with his feet exposed. Someone had stolen his shoes. No one would have taken those old perforated boots if we had all had decent pairs of shoes.

It was around eleven o'clock when a bell in one of the watchtowers rang. We all ran to the head of the ramp. Obviously, those who could dashed forward, while others struggled to keep up, including our gallery's team. When we got to the ramp, I was paralyzed with horror. Standing there were Gazdov, Goranov, Gogov, Captain

Neshev, Vutov, Krǔstev, Yozo the Valaque, and all the policemen and guards. They were all carrying their clubs and were shouting as they divided us into groups. In front of the ramp, a train with twenty-five wagons had come to a halt. The piles of stone had to be carried by hand to the wagons. Near some of the wagons, wood planks were propped up against the ramp. The wagons passed by, filled with gravel. The large stones were tossed from the top of the ramp wall. If one of the stones accidentally fell on top of the track, the guards took it for an act of sabotage. The guilty person was beaten to within an inch of his life. The loading itself was a real spectacle: ten or so prisoners running and stumbling with huge rocks in their arms, while guards flailed furiously at anyone within arm's reach and screamed, "Faster! Stop dawdling! Faster!"

I didn't escape this gauntlet. Gazdov decided that the stone I was carrying was not big enough—especially, he said, since I'd just arrived and still had all my strength—and he struck me on the back. I ran like a madman up the ramp and tried to avoid the powerful blows from these brutes. In fifteen or twenty minutes, the train was loaded and the bell sounded again. We had to step back. At that moment, I saw that at the end of the ramp there were also women, who were now heading back up a path. Obviously, they had loaded the last wagons. A normal person could never have imagined this spectacle.

Once it was over, we climbed back down to the quarry. My hands, which were now open wounds, were hideous to look at. The blood was mixed with mud and dirt—once it clotted, it was extremely painful to remove. My entire body was terribly bruised, and the pain sent me reeling. I could hardly walk, and my clothing fell off in shreds each time I brushed against the rocks. When I reached the gallery, there were only four of us. The nice Jewish fellow was no longer there. Nobody knew what had become of him. We stopped for a minute, but then the bell sounded again. Two barrels filled with boiled beans, already cold, had been brought. The soup was ladled out into our bowls, and we sat down to eat it, indifferent to the cold. But we had only a couple of minutes of rest. We went back to work, and once again the falling of sledgehammers, picks, and clubs was heard, along with the ranting, the curses, and the threats. All the guards and officers were there. They took turns beating the prisoners, and were followed by the brigade leaders. The latter watched the officers closely. If the officers devoted more time to beating a particular victim, then the brigade chiefs would finish him off. It seemed to be a tacit agreement between them.

The bell sounded a third time that afternoon. It was the warning that the Lovech-Troyan train was approaching and that we had to lie down and hide ourselves. The passengers peered out the windows, straining for a glimpse of the famous concentration camp. I still wonder how it is that people knew back then about the camp's existence, yet today insist that they didn't know anything about it.[6]

Toward nine o'clock at night, we were ordered to line up in rows. The armed guards surrounded us, joined by the brigade leaders, who were carrying clubs. They forced us to take one another by the arm, and the convoy of raggedy men was ready to move. But the order was suddenly given to all the new arrivals to step out from their rows. My heart nearly stopped. I told myself that they were going to kill us under the cover of darkness.

Four trembling wretches dressed in rags stepped forward ... an awful sight awaited us. A canvas sack had been thrown into the handcart that had been brought that morning. The metal strip that tied it shut glowed dully in the darkness. We were ordered to take the cart and push it along the rows. We started out, bent over by the weight and our feet dragging in the mud. It was 19 December, Saint Nikolas Day. People in the world outside were celebrating the holiday, while I was pushing a cart that contained the body of that likable Jewish man. God has forgiven him. But will He ever pardon those who killed him?

6. Another prisoner recounts, "When the morning train passed, toward ten o'clock or so, we were forced to lie down behind the piles of stone, gravel, or sand. But when the evening train passed, at five o'clock, we had to quit the quarry and run, all the while beaten so that we'd run faster, to the camp esplanade. There a Gypsy played a ... drum, I believe. And we were ordered to dance. When the train passengers waved, we were forced to wave back. As soon as the train passed and the last car had disappeared, the music stopped and the stick blows again started. We then returned to our work in the quarry" (*The Survivors*).

Gogov, Gazdov, and Goranov were waiting for us at the entrance of our barbed-wire encampment. One of them was sifting the group for those men who had not fulfilled the quota in the galleries. The brigade chiefs made their reports. Upon hearing the number of my gallery called out, I stepped forward. One of the policemen chased us with his club to the guardhouse. Inside, Adjutant Vutov was waiting with a rubber tube in his hand. He ordered us to drop our pants and lie down on our stomachs. We obeyed. While he beat us, we had to count out loud. One, two, three ... We then began to bellow like wounded animals.

When we crawled back to the esplanade, the other prisoners were already eating their evening soup, which had been leftover from lunch. They were eating on their feet in the cold. We weren't given much time and were called for evening roll call. The scene from the previous night was repeated. We were placed along three sides of the rectangle; we were counted by the guards.... During this moment of calm, I could observe the sad scene that surrounded me. I noticed a few old men without shoes. They had instead wrapped their feet in rags, which were now soaked and weighed down on their feet.

It was past ten o'clock when Gazdov and Goranov stepped in front of us. Indescribable screaming began, and prisoners' names were called out. One by one, poor wretches stepped forward and were so brutally beaten that they fell moaning to the ground. Accusations, curses, and beatings continued till late in the night. Men standing near me were dozing on their feet, leaning against one another for support. After two hours or so had passed, the brigade leaders took us to our barracks. We threw ourselves onto the straw mattresses filled with bedbugs and lice. Almost immediately, the smell of gangrene filled the air. One small stove was lit in the corner. Near it, drying their wet socks and clothes, congregated the prisoner elite—those mercenaries paid to kill. Everybody else immediately fell asleep without exchanging a single word.

That was my first day at Lovech. My first day of reeducation under the auspices of Section 0789, Bureau of State Security at the Ministry of the Interior. The first day of my struggle against death.

The following morning, and the months that followed, repeated what had happened that first day. On my way to the toilet, I saw a canvas sack thrown against the back wall. It contained the body of the poor Jewish man that I'd carried.[7] At first I felt sick, but then I envied him. Nobody bothered about him any longer, and he was sleeping tranquilly. But this sleep was to be disturbed one last time. His body was taken to Work Site No. 5 at Belene, the terminus for the hearse that carried these wretched corpses. Yes, the pigpens at Belene became our Père Lachaise.[8]

———

Ragtag convoys to the quarries in the heart of winter, incessant beatings, carts laden with stone bound for the thirty train cars, handcarts laden with heavy canvas bags on the return to camp, the evening roll call. . . . Above all, there was the struggle against death. In Section 0789 death constantly hovered above us.

One winter's day the cold was especially fierce. The bell sounded toward three o'clock in the afternoon, interrupting our routine. We all wondered what had happened. Suddenly, we were ordered to leave the quarry and run toward the barracks. Stick blows rained down upon us, forcing us to run as fast as we could. Hand in hand with our fellow prisoners, paralyzed by the fear of the unknown, we started out. Poor, naive fellow that I was, I secretly hoped that they had taken pity on us because of the cold. We halted

7. Here is a witness's account concerning another Jewish prisoner:

I was in the same brigade with Ariko, a Jew who had gold-filled teeth. When he told us one morning that he was to push the handcart and canvas sack, we realized that he was going to be killed that day. He was forced to push the wagon by himself, and Goranov hit him on the head with his cudgel. He split open his skull and his brain splattered everywhere. They left his body outside, and that night put it in the sack. The next morning, Gogov ordered me and some others to load the cart. The sack was undone, and Ariko's head, which jutted out, was ... well, it didn't look like a human head. There were no teeth left in his mouth. That same night they were all pulled out for the gold! (*The Survivors*)

8. Translator's note: Père Lachaise is the cemetery in northeastern Paris that is home to the famous and obscure, as well as the site of the massacre in 1871 of hundreds of participants in the Paris Commune.

before the gate to the camp and waited. Gogov, Gazdov, Goranov appeared along with the rest of the guards, armed with machine guns and clubs. Shouting furiously, they ordered us to line up. A cordon of murderous guards took its place some twenty meters away and herded us outside the camp. We were forced to run across a field covered with a thick layer of snow to the Osŭm River, which was a good six to seven hundred meters away.

While running I asked myself if they had the intention to make us bathe in the river. It was hardly the weather for such an activity, but these sadists were capable of anything. Upon reaching the river, I saw that it was frozen and that my hypothesis was wrong. Axes were given to a few of us, with the order to break the ice into pieces between thirty and forty centimeters thick. They were, quite simply, blocks of ice. We each had to take one of these ice blocks in our arms and run with it back to the camp. A huge hole had been dug near the police barracks, and we had to place a layer of ice in it, followed by a layer of straw. This foot race to the river and back again was repeated several times. The pit was to serve during the summer as a refrigerator for the guards.

My hands, already covered with wounds, stuck to the ice. I tried to use my chest to support the blocks of ice, but my shirt stiffened as hard as wood. I was grabbing the ice by the fringe of my coat, but with each passing minute I felt myself growing as cold as the ice and felt that the end was near. It was the clubbings I received as I ran to the river and back that kept my frozen blood circulating. We finished filling the pit in two or three hours. It was yet one more battle with death.

We lined up with our clothes frozen to our bodies for roll call. For nearly an hour, we stood there as Gazdov relentlessly barked out his advice. A few of the frozen prisoners were rebuked, and we were then permitted to lie down. Our clothing began to thaw on our bodies and had the effect of a wet compress. I fell into a deep sleep.

At morning roll call the next day, we were sent off to work. Coughing and spitting up, we marched off in the darkness. Fever and bronchial pneumonia, added to the infected sores of the prisoners, were hardly reasons to rest at the camp. The nurse, Zhoro, who was from Varna,[9] had bandages and cotton, mercurochrome and iodine, but they were reserved for those whose limbs had been crushed or torn off.

—

One particular January morning seemed to be just another day in our bleak existence, but there was a certain tension in the air. Before we began loading the train at the quarry, the level of tension became unbearable. Prisoners were being beaten in all the galleries. Vutov was a madman, screaming that the "chiefs" were arriving and that we had to work faster. Puzzled, I wondered who these new "chiefs" could be. The ones we had were already more than enough for us.

At a certain point, I noticed a group of people at the rim of the quarry, at a spot that had been cleared by the female prisoners. Our three assassins stood among them, but there were two others I didn't recognize. One of them had a limp, while the other, with a preening air, watched us with his chest puffed out, like a father proudly observing his sons. Sent by Sofia on an official mission, the presence of these men boosted the rhythm of work and the beatings to an unimaginable level. The train was loaded in a record time. The brigade leaders shouted that the quota in the galleries had been increased. All of us, alive or half-alive, dug into the rock and loaded the carts in a matter of seconds. We remained in the quarry until late that same night. When we were then led back to the camp, I saw a pale blue Ford with Sofia license plates parked in front of the gate. Clearly, it was the car that had brought the VIPs. It was only after we were given our dinner and had a few moments to ourselves that I was able to ask the veteran prisoners about our visitors. I was told that it was Colonel Chakŭrov and Mircho Spasov[10] (I cannot remember what his officer grade was at the time). This cruel man started to visit us often, twice a month. His presence was painful for all the prisoners. An official envoy of the bigwigs in Sofia, he spread terror from the moment he arrived. Everything would increase: the

9. See his account on pages 133–38.
10. See his account on pages 159–63.

quotas, the beatings, the horror, the canvas sacks dumped by the toilets.... It was only thanks to the war I had declared on death, a pure animal instinct, that I stayed alive during those wintry days in January 1961.

—

Evening roll call. Rumor had it that there would be newcomers, including a rich fellow from Sofia. At least this was the gossip while we were on the esplanade eating our repulsive soup. As soon as the new prisoner arrived, he was beaten. During the roll call, Gazdov "explained" the camp rules to him. Big and strong, this man had all it takes to put up a fight. Before going to sleep that night, I heard him tell his neighbors that he had just bought a Renault Dauphine at the Central Store in Sofia. While turning the car keys in his hand, he said he didn't understand why he was here. Perhaps he never understood why. Over the short period of about a week, death kept a relentless watch on him. He was never given a break. We didn't work together, so I don't really know what his days were like. As for the nights, he was tortured. Finally, one day the rumor spread that he'd been killed. We saw a canvas sack near the toilets that night. His name was Ivan Karadochev, and he was given his pass for Work Site No. 5 at Belene. I hope there was a witness to say who gave Ivan the last and final blow. As for the first of the fatal blows, there are many witnesses.

After having sent the one letter I was permitted, I received a package from my parents. How this came to be I'll never know, for this happened to one prisoner out of a hundred. Though it was the only one I ever received during my imprisonment, the package was terribly important. My dear mother packed inside a fur vest that I put under my old rags. Not only did it protect me from the cold, but, more important, from the stick blows. This package tied me to life, to all that was good.[11] It meant faith, support, goodness: things so

11. Packages received by prisoners were often an excuse for additional punishment and humiliations. One woman recounts that she was forced to burn in public the contents of her package. Another prisoner asserts, "The guards took great pleasure in forbidding someone who had just received a package from eating the food inside; they'd be killed before they could touch it" (*The Survivors*).

important in this hell. I was revitalized by the warmth of my family and, for a short while, able to forget evil. I forgot Gazdov, Goranov, Dimitŭr Tsvetkov (who had taken a particular "liking" to me), those miserable jackals Slavcho of Sofia, Andrey of Haskovo, Levordashki of Sofia, Tsanko and Shakho.

There were six days in a workweek, each day lasting fifteen hours. On Sundays we worked only to noon. In the afternoon, unable to escape the cold air, we tried to take care of personal affairs. Those bloodied by beatings or covered with gangrene rested inside the stinking barracks. One Sunday I was trying to wash my socks without soap in the freezing water when I saw Shakho, screaming like a madman, leading another victim behind the barbed wire. He cruelly beat the poor wretch. I left my socks on the ground and went over to the new victim. He was a relatively young man with a pleasant and intelligent expression. He seemed to be from Sofia. Veteran prisoner that I now was, I looked at him with pity. I was no longer one of the "newcomers." I was known as Little Colas.

After being given some rags, the new arrival was assigned to flatten the ground of the esplanade with a heavy roller. The brigade chief Andrey walked behind, periodically hitting him with his heavy club. The man with the roller would twist and try to run. Several brigade leaders took turns at this task—Slavcho, Shakho, Tsvetkov—while the poor fellow struggled and slaved away. We cast furtive looks toward the esplanade and exchanged a few words. Some of the older Sofians identified the man as Sasha "Dearheart," the famous violinist who played at the restaurant in the Bulgaria Hotel. Sasha Nikolov (his real name) had brought along his violin: clearly, he didn't know where he was being sent. At the evening inspection, some fifteen torturers had a field day. One after the other, they hammered away at the musician as if they were in a relay race. They were absolutely beside themselves. What was the explanation? What had this man done?

We were herded back to the barracks. Those who knew Sasha helped him to bed. Astonishingly, he managed to smile. At a certain point, he leaned up against a pole and asked that he be given his violin. He played a bit, enough to remind us of the outside world.

Enough to bring tears to our eyes. He then fell asleep, or perhaps lost consciousness—I cannot say.

At breakfast the following morning, it was whispered that the musician was "in the sack." It seems that he had carried his fate with him in the form of an envelope sealed with red wax. The obedient dogs had followed the enclosed orders. Who killed him? The first one who struck him? Or the last one? Or the ones in the middle? Or the unknown officials who had sent the order? Let us hope that the truth will come to light one day.[12]

Winter, work, and beatings fully occupied our time. Each minute that passed was a minute of life gained. But death walked among us, hovered above us, and grabbed us. It would then relax its grip, only to pursue us again. I no longer thought about those who had pronounced my death sentence. They paled in importance next to my struggle to survive. While I was at Lovech, they probably were receiving official prizes and medals for their struggle against enemies of the state. Forgive me, my Lord . . .

During the harsh winter of 1961, the female prisoners, whom we glimpsed from time to time, must have numbered about one hundred. They left for work every morning at the same time as did our brigade, but marched ahead of us. Like us, they were guarded by police carrying heavy clubs. Their chiefs were Yulia the "Beauty," Totka (the wife of Captain Neshev), Kina, and, of course, a female prisoner deliberately chosen for her qualities, Lilyana. They all carried clubs. The women were near a large rock, clearing the layer

12. Alexandre Nikolov, known as Sasha "Dearheart" (*Sladura*), stayed in the memories of many natives of Sofia. Born into a well-off family in 1915, he studied at the Italian School and the French College. He went on to the Prague Conservatory and, beginning in 1940, played in a symphony orchestra. After the war, his social and political "profile" led him to play in restaurant orchestras, especially at the Bulgaria Hotel. His sparkling personality endeared him to audiences (his nickname was due to his inability to remember the names of all his girlfriends, calling them all "dear heart"). He was also celebrated for his storytelling. At times, he was even invited by the chiefs of state, like Dimitrov, Chervenkov, and Zhivkov, to entertain them with his amusing stories and violin playing. Apparently, it was his storytelling that led to his deportation to Lovech. The police telegram to his mother announcing his death attributed it to a heart attack. (Information taken from I. Slavov's *Zlatnata reshetka* [Sofia, 1991].)

of topsoil in the quarry. The soil was two meters thick. They dug into the frozen earth with the help of picks, then filled up the carts. I heard that their quota was four cubic meters. Like the men, they were beaten daily. Beatings without end, without reason. One winter's day a woman threw herself from the boulder, which was twenty meters high, and fell into the gallery where my team was working. She was probably at the end of her rope. Her despair was easy to understand. You see, one day we were again standing in front of the camp gate for not having filled the quota. It's then that I also tasted the cruelty of Yulia. Upon being ordered into the guardhouse, I saw Yulia, facing Adjutant Yozo, with a rubber tube in her hands. When I entered, she screamed at me to lie stomach-down on the floor. Terrible blows began to fall, and I moaned from pain. At a certain point, she kicked me in the stomach with her booted foot, and yelled at me to return to the barracks. After this incident, I was certain that all of the guards were assigned to this camp in order to kill.

It's perhaps opportune to mention something that most human beings could hardly imagine. Ramadan Dokov was the brother of the most devoted assassin in the camp hierarchy, Shakho-Quasimodo. Hardly a day passed that Ramadan, a sturdy Gypsy, was not beaten by his own brother. What often struck me was that Shakho worked him over in front of Gazdov, Goranov, and Gogov in order to show his complete and utter loyalty to them.

Two other brothers from Haskovo were also brought in. One of the them, Mitko, survived, while the other, according to the established pattern, was put in the sack in a horrible fashion under my own eyes. For a long time, Mitko spoke to no one. Afraid that he would go crazy, Gazdov named him a brigade chief, and he was given a club. But did that ease his pain? It's impossible to say, for he never hit anyone. The officers' primitive minds convinced them that they could thus absolve their faults. . . . How could one ever believe that, by giving a club to someone, you'd make him forget the evil he's endured?

Toward the end of January, I saw a new arrival on the esplanade shortly before evening roll call. He seemed to be as young as I was. Brought from Sofia, he was shoeless and sockless. Since we slept together in the same bed, we soon became friends. He worked at the "silos." We'd talk together a little at night before going to sleep, but weariness would soon come over us. When we meet even today, we always find something new to say about our experience. The impressions made by the camp were so powerful, and the opportunities to talk about them so few. His name is Bozhidar Petrov.[13] He often complained about his brigade chief, Blagoy Gaytanski of Plovdiv, also known as the Donkey. Strong and bald, this killer had been handpicked by Gazdov. However, Konstantin Peshev supervised the work of the brigade chiefs in that same quarry. He was a generous individual who saved the life of many men, including Bozhidar's.

A few days after Bozhidar's arrival at the camp, an unusual evening roll call took place. Ivan Bŭrzakov of Sofia was led out from a row of prisoners. After being beaten by Goranov and Gazdov, Ivan was tied to a post by Adjutant Yozo under the glare of a spot-light. It was minus twenty degrees centigrade. We looked at one another, dumbfounded by this new inquisitorial method. Gazdov ordered that a hose be attached to a sink faucet and brought to him. He started to spray the wretched man, who turned into a block of ice under our eyes. He remained tied up all night, periodically watered down with the hose. To our great astonishment, he was still alive the following day. It was only that evening that we saw the canvas sack near the latrine. The struggle against death sometimes works miracles.

During one morning inspection, a prisoner was found to be missing. The brigade chiefs ran up and down through the barracks. They discovered the missing man: he was still in his bunk. Thinking the old man was asleep, they screamed at him to get up, but he couldn't. He had plunged a knife into his heart at night. The canvas sack containing his body remained near the toilets for a long time, and we filed by to pay our respects.

A new visit paid from Sofia by Spasov and Chakŭrov raised the quota to seventy-five carts. This was impossible for most of us

13. His account is on pages 50–54, 62–63, and 109–12.

to meet. I was punished in front of the camp gate nearly every night. One afternoon, a doctor from Sofia was brought to the quarry. His name was Marinski. It was said that he had been the Party's secretary general at the hospital, where he had been denounced by colleagues. He had been worked over and was as pale as a sheet. For a short while we worked together in the same gallery, but the poor man couldn't reach the unrealistic quota. But there was another gallery where the quota was always met, thanks to a young giant by the name of Boris Gikov.[14] The doctor was able to join Gikov's team. But it mattered little even if one worked like the devil and was as strong as a rock. Goranov's stick flashed down one day on Boris. He had been slandered by a brigade chief, who said that Boris had sworn to hang Goranov from a willow tree if he ever left the camp alive. Boris was still unconscious when he was taken back to the camp in a cart. We thought he was dead, but by some miracle he survived.

One freezing morning in February, I heard my name called out during an inspection. "Little Colas, step forward!" An indescribable terror overwhelmed me. As if in a dream, I stood in front of the row. In his brutal, insane manner, Gazdov screamed at me to undress. When I was stripped to my waist, the murderer began to work me over with blows. He yelled that wise guys, like myself, who wore fur vests under their clothes would get what they deserved. Anticipating my end, I silently wished goodbye to my loved ones. I was numb all over, and the row of prisoners began to spin around me. I must have fallen unconscious, for at a certain point I heard a voice that seemed to rise from the depths of the earth and ordered me back into line. I lifted my head and saw Gazdov's bared teeth right next to my ear. He was shouting with incredible force. I'd barely picked up my clothes and dragged myself back into line when I was stunned by another blow. This time it came from someone in front of me. I saw Andrey smiling with satisfaction. Perhaps he was the one who told Gazdov about my secret. This was how I came to be parted from my vest and all the physical and emotional warmth it brought.

14. His account is on pages 45–46, 55–60, and 97–100.

The indescribable pain from the beating kept me from sleeping. Since Bozhidar was deep asleep, I couldn't share my fears with him. I was haunted by the question of whether I'd now survive the rest of the winter.

At roll call the next morning, Gazdov once again appeared. The monster ordered two men to step forward. They were the Grigorovs from Sofia, a father and his son. They were both very intelligent and likable, easygoing and inseparable. Gazdov ordered them each to take a handcart, chuckling that these same carts would bring their bodies back to camp that night. He then pulled out a hand mirror in which he customarily looked at himself to smooth down his hair. Showing it to the Grigorovs, he announced, "Look at yourselves for the last time!"

I didn't see which quarry the two condemned men had been sent to work, but when we returned that night, two canvas sacks were loaded onto the two carts, exactly as Gazdov had said they would. After having seen so many corpses in so short a time, I wondered about the identity of the men who stood behind these brutes. Who gave them the authorization to dispose so easily of human lives? Were there no decent men in the government to control these criminals?

Alas, each day brought yet more canvas sacks loaded onto carts. One day there would be a single sack, the next day several sacks. We didn't know all of victims, nor did we see how they all died exactly. It was only by the number of sacks piled by the latrine that we had an idea of the body count. It was in a sack that the corpse of a very nice fellow was brought in one day. He had come from Belene the day our camp was created. His name was Anani, from Pernik. He had a welcoming smile and was an intelligent and quiet man. He wasn't the only one: we were all quiet, since none of us wanted to stand out.

Death walked among us and could pay a visit at any moment. And the visits were repeated. Roll call, work, bell, train, lunch, work, bell, dinner, roll call, sleep. For each of these commas, you could quite easily and without hesitation substitute the word "death."

We had loaded the umpteenth train. The bell had already started to sound, signaling us to step away. We all did so, with the exception of Ivan Khinkov of Pleven. He threw himself under the wheels of the train. A recent arrival in the camp, he was eighteen or nineteen years old. The train stopped and Ivan was pulled out, but without his two legs. However, the boy was still alive. Gogov and Gazdov began to howl like maniacs. How dare this bastard make a mess of the work schedule! But they didn't dare touch him. Instead, they continued to shower unbelievable curses upon this poor, suffering fellow. At that very moment, there arrived the assistant to these murderers, Levordashki from Sofia. He was carrying a huge hammer, the one we used to break rocks. I closed my eyes and remembered once again that we'd been sent to this camp in order to better ourselves. Here we were, in the middle of the twentieth century, in Bulgaria, a civilized nation devoted, it was thought, to freedom and justice under the reign of Communism. . . . Levordashki lifted the hammer and brought it down on Ivan's chest. Gogov and Gazdov sighed with relief. My eyes opened, but I couldn't believe what I saw.

The month of March arrived. The spring weather warmed the ground, and the camp grew busier. Groups of prisoners from all over Bulgaria began to arrive. Between ten and fifteen people entered through the gate every day. One day in March a friend from Sofia, Emil Pǔrvanov (Emo), appeared in the camp. He, too, had been called in for an identification check. He was sixteen. The camp very quickly filled with innocent men who didn't have a single black mark against them. They were grabbed arbitrarily and sacrificed on the altar of totalitarianism. By the beginning of the summer, there were about 1,500 men in the camp. Too many to get to know. No one knew who had arrived, when he arrived, and when he was killed. The canvas sacks near the toilets multiplied in number. There were now more than ten each day. They began to stink in the heat, yet the hearse idled.[15] Two or three clubs were broken against our

15. Many of the prisoners have sharp memories of this truck, to which we'll return later (pages 154–55, n. 2). Everyone agrees that sacks containing the corpses were piled up behind the toilets, sometimes for several days and until there were

backs every day. One man was given the specific task to carve the clubs from dogwood trees, which are particularly hard.

During this period, one man especially stood out: Dimitŭr Tsvetkov, nicknamed the Invisible Man. He was Gazdov's favorite subordinate. He had murdered more than fifty people upon orders from above. But the old principle of murderers' never trusting fellow murderers applied to Section 0789. Tsvetkov was accused of stealing meat from the kitchen and was sentenced to the death quarry. He had barely started to work when the vengeance started. Even we noticed it, though we were half-dead ourselves. This treatment was welcomed by his superiors. After just four hours of work and horrendous beatings, Tsvetkov stuck his hand under the wheels of a wagon. All of his fingers were crushed. But even then he wasn't spared the constant beating. Before the evening roll call, he was on the esplanade with his hand completely swollen. The gangrene was spreading quickly. During the inspection, Gazdov ordered him to come forward and announced Tsvetkov's misdeed (he had eaten two pieces of meat). He then began to pound the murderer's back. All the while, Gazdov explained to him that such behavior wouldn't do at all, that it was intolerable that one man should steal meat while others worked. We all knew that this display of humanitarian sentiment was nothing more than the pot's calling the kettle black. Early the next morning, Tsvetkov, his body a mass of bruises and his hand covered with gangrene, had climbed to the top of the quarry to push rocks over the edge with his crowbar. Upon reaching the top, he dove off head first. He was thrown half-dead into a sack. No one wanted to push the cart back to the camp that night. The task was given to four wretched men who had all been personally beaten by Tsvetkov. Perhaps this time around the pigs ate with a heartier appetite.

---

twenty—all of this due to the desire to save gasoline. This explains the odor of decaying bodies, which clung to the sacks, which were returned empty from Belene and recycled. The rest of the time the truck was used to carry provisions for the camp. One prisoner recounts, "More than once I ate bread stained with human blood, since the vehicle used to transport the corpses also carried our bread" (Kosta Kostov, *Den,* 9 April 1990).

We were the ones—the very same hooligans that the residents of Lovech held in such horror—who built the better part of their town. Beginning in April, there were from ten to fifteen work sites across the city. The offices of the Communist Party and the Ministry of the Interior, the interior minister's residence, the "Stratech" work site, the Party's meeting hall, Melta, Factory No. 14, the asphalt factory, the motorcycle race course, the stadium, Bahovitsa, the city quarry, the Slivek sand quarry, the Municipal Council building, the building supply depot, the sawmill in the town of Tcherni Osŭm. Thanks to its ties with the first secretary of the Party, Mircho Spasov, Lovech had the privilege to be built by prisoners. At least for this I owe a debt of gratitude: after four months in the death quarry I was reassigned to the outside work sites. At most of these sites, we weren't beaten during the day and worked with civilian laborers. Those accused of "minor crimes" were usually assigned to these construction sites. Not that this work wasn't dangerous, mind you. The briefest of conversations with a civilian or a single cigarette accepted from an outsider meant a beating during evening roll call. Moreover, we'd be reassigned to the "great quarry."

One summer day, a newcomer from Sofia was brought in. He was my age and his name was Boyko (Jacky). He had been sent to the small quarry near the "silos," where his brigade chief was Blago the Donkey. A couple of days after his arrival, he was brutally beaten by Blago. Jacky was brought back to the camp in a sack. This was how Darcho the Frenchman, from Pleven, also came to his end. He was twenty-two years old.

One day they brought in a young boy named Lyubcho, who was from Gabrovo. He was the nephew of a Party member of a departmental committee. From what we understood, he'd been hauled in at the request of his father. It seems he wanted to give his son a good fright for a few days. The poor boy was terribly young, not more than sixteen or seventeen. Gazdov did his very best to "give him a fright." At the end of four or five days, the boy was carried back to camp in a sack. A heartbreaking scene took place at the camp gates ten days later, when the parents arrived in a luxurious official car to reclaim the body of their "reeducated" son. They weren't even allowed to take the body, though they stayed a few days outside the camp.

There undoubtedly were several similar cases, but after a long day we hardly had the strength to talk among ourselves. Besides, silence was the rule—especially on the outside work sites. We had to work without uttering a single word and with our eyes turned to the ground. We were taken to work in trucks guarded by three policemen armed with machine guns, forced to keep our heads bowed so that we couldn't make eye contact with chance passersby. This was how we crossed the city. As we passed by, the townspeople would cry, "Here come the hoodlums! Murderers!"

Returning from work one night, we saw a young man sprawled out on the esplanade. He was from Varna. The men from the "silos" reported that a huge rock had fallen that same morning and crushed both his legs. He was left on the esplanade, half-conscious and moaning from pain. Gazdov wouldn't authorize a trip to the hospital. The poor boy remained in that state until the next day, when the necessary authorization arrived from Sofia. By that time, gangrene had spread through his legs, and they were both amputated. Once he recovered, he was sent back to the quarry. But his wife was subsequently contacted, and she came to the camp and brought him home.

All of us were obsessed by a single thought: to escape this hell. But it was practically impossible. If one failed, the consequences were horrifying: it was either the firing squad or being clubbed to death. The first one to attempt an escape was quickly found by huge, specially trained dogs. He was in a sack the next day. The second one to try, Zdravko from Burgas, was working at the Party's meeting hall site in Lovech. With his hammer, he hit the policeman who was guarding him, took his gun, and fled. Due to the influence of Zdravko's brother, the public prosecutor's office in Lovech refused to send him back to the camp. He was tried and found guilty. Nevertheless, many things about the "death camp" came to light during the trial.

Traycho, known as the Little Serb, escaped from the quarry in mysterious circumstances and managed to reach Sofia. His escape served as a pretext to physically punish all the prisoners without exception. Those who were closest to him were really put through the mill. When they left for the quarry, they were carrying sacks over their shoulders. This was meant to serve as an example.

In Sofia, Traycho committed a robbery in order to be caught and tried in court. He wanted to make public the horrors of the camp. The comrades, however, didn't fall for the trap and ordered Traycho back to the camp. Sensing what was in store for him, the Little Serb swallowed the handle of an aluminum spoon while being held in a guardhouse in Sofia. He was operated on in the Ministry of Interior's hospital. While recuperating, he managed to recount to others the horrors at Lovech. Someone from the Yugoslavian embassy also visited him.

But nothing happened. Once back on his feet, Traycho was again ordered back to Lovech. While being held in the guardhouse at Pleven, the stubborn Serb succeeded in swallowing yet a second spoon.... It was at the hospital in Pleven that yet more details concerning the concentration camp were revealed. The secrecy surrounding Section 0789 began to be pierced. As a result, the order came down from Sofia that though he was to be sent back to the camp, Traycho wasn't to be harmed. When he returned, we hadn't the slightest idea of what he'd been through, and no one suspected the eventual impact of his heroic act. During the evening roll call, Gazdov ordered that Traycho remain at the work site on the pretext that he was still sick.

However, terrible days followed. Several more young men were killed. There was Pencho from Burgas, who was twenty. Following two months of brutal treatment, he was reduced to a wreck who could hardly stand on his own two feet. Sharo, who also was from Burgas, was the one who finished him off. Another young boy from Burgas, Blagoy, was also horribly beaten by Sharo. By some miracle, however, Blagoy survived....

This wasn't the only miracle: at the end of October 1961, Gazdov, Gogov, and Goranov suddenly disappeared from the camp. So, too, did their assistant assassins Vutov, Yozo, Krŭstev, and Captain

Neshev. We wondered what had happened. Was it possible that there was a public groundswell of revulsion? Had the revelations of the Little Serb done their work? Or was it that these particular assassins were too steeped in blood and had to be replaced by a new set? I now know what had happened, but at the time we trembled in the face of the unknown. It was actually very simple. General Mircho Spasov, who sensed that the truth was getting out, had decided to act first and control the unfolding of events.

Due to lack of personnel, evening roll call was led by old Ivan Panteleev, the only policeman who never used his club. Then Colonel Alexandrov appeared before us.[16] Regional director of State Security at Lovech, Alexandrov announced that, starting tomorrow, we'd work only eight hours a day. Moreover, he had secretly ordered the guards to put away their clubs.

The first day of November was incredible! Calm reigned everywhere. Everyone worked. There were no beatings. Emo and I were then working at the construction site for the interior minister's villa. We were making a terrace where vines would be planted. From the top of the building . . . we could see the camp's esplanade and toilets, where until a few days before the bodies in canvas sacks were still kept. Minister Tsankov[17] would have a lovely view when he came to relax in a villa built with the blood of so many men! The stones were brought from the "silos," carried by men who ran to the very top. . . . As for those who worked in the villa's underground shelter, it was thought that they'd all be killed. It was even thought that Willy Tadger, who served as architect, would be killed. It was definitely a miracle that we survived.

I imagine that a good number of important bureaucrats have stayed in that villa; perhaps some of them still work in the Ministry of the Interior. Let them know (if some of them somehow do not yet know it) how they've come to enjoy this view. Let them remember the thousands of victims—the deaths of us "hoodlums"—who built these pleasant surroundings.

16. See his account on pages 153–57.
17. See his account on pages 163–64.

A blue-hatted officer accompanied by Alexandrov turned up in November: he was the new director. Later that same month, a group of officials arrived at the camp. Apparently a commission of sorts, they wanted to speak to each of the prisoners individually and examine our wounds and scars. We were nevertheless too afraid to reveal the truth. (It should be noted that this was not the Boris Velchev Commission.)

I'd just spent my eleventh month in the camp. Apart from the package that followed my first letter, I'd had no news of my family. Every month I received one hundred leva, which was the sole connection I had with them. An ancient machine was brought in to sterilize our clothing. Lice and bedbugs crawled by the hundreds over our bodies. Some of us were given slightly newer clothing, and Doctor Marinski began to treat the infected wounds with medicine that may have been basic but had never before been available. We worked a great deal, but at least were no longer beaten. The food remained the same noxious brew as before. The roll calls were shortened. A winter no less bitter than the last one began to settle in. We rarely loaded the trains. In the beginning of December, we saw women prisoners going to Skravena for medical treatment. A number of them were immediately liberated. Something was clearly in the works. Most important, however, was that our murderers had left.

During morning roll call at the end of January 1962, Ivan Panteleev read out the names of Little Colas, Emil Pŭrvanov, and Traycho the Little Serb. We were to remain behind in camp and keep ourselves ready. I felt my heart skip a beat. After the others left for their work sites, we were called, one by one, into Gazdov's old office and told that we were free. We had to sign a statement in which we swore that we'd never speak to anyone under any pretext whatsoever about what we had gone through and seen.

In the storeroom we found the clothes we had been wearing when we arrived at the camp. Three adjutants put us into a waiting car and took us to the station in Levski. We were each given a money order and then put on the train to Sofia. We were told to reply, should anyone on the train ask who we were, that we worked

at the local sawmill. This is how I won my precious freedom. God
alone helped us in our struggle against death.

———

Up to the end of March, group after group of innocent men who
had been condemned to die in Section 0789 were liberated. There
remained, in the end, about 100 to 150 men at the camp, including
the brigade chiefs and those prisoners with criminal records. It was
at that moment, purged of everyone but brutes and criminals, that
the camp was investigated by the Velchev Commission. There was
no trace left by those monsters Gazdov, Gogov, and Goranov. In a
humanitarian gesture, the Party's political headquarters closed the
camp. This happened at the end of April 1962.

In my opinion, more than 1,500 people were sent to this
camp, and a few hundred were killed.

When I returned home, no one could believe their eyes. My
mother, who had been in mourning, nearly fainted. My father stared
at me and could not believe it was me, especially since he had already
lodged dozens of fruitless complaints with the Interior Ministry.
They had lost all hope that they'd ever again see me alive. Every three
months, the packages they tried to send to me were returned. Same
thing for the letters. Their only hope was based on the fact that the
money orders got through. Upon seeing the scars on my back and
blisters on my hands, my mother was unable to sleep for months. My
twisted fingers were just three quarters their original length, and my
calluses were nearly a centimeter thick. My legs were covered in varicose veins, yet I was only nineteen years old. When I went to see the
doctor for the varicose veins, he wanted to operate immediately. I
refused, and this is why I now suffer from phlebitis.

The day after my return home, I was called to Police Station
No. 6, where my passport was returned. Officials from the Bureau
of State Security asked me what I had done during the last thirteen
months. I replied that I had a shock that led to a form of amnesia,
and limited myself to showing them my hands. Don't forget that I
had signed that statement.... One couldn't expect anything good
from these people. Perhaps they were checking to see if I'd already
forgotten....

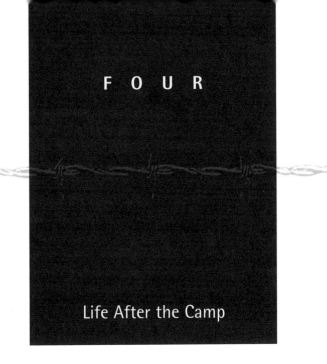

F O U R

Life After the Camp

BORIS GIKOV

My nerves were seriously weakened by the two and one-half years I spent in the camp. In order to get some much-needed rest, I didn't return to work at the start of 1962....

Eventually I met Elena and we were married. I was hired at the Vaptsarov Mills, where I worked as a mill hand. Family life went smoothly, since Elena was a fine housewife and made to be an ideal mother.... I changed jobs and went to work at a factory that produced pharmaceutical and beauty products.

However, one morning—the very same day as my birthday— two plainclothesmen came to the house and, though they didn't have a warrant, searched it. I was then summoned once again for a "small identification check" at police headquarters. I was brought into the police chief's office, where I found a number of plainclothesmen waiting. One of them asked how it was that I managed to leave the camp alive. I answered that I did the work that was asked of me, despite all the torture and beatings. A second cop said I may have worked a lot, but maybe I had talked a lot too. Why else would they receive the order to have me permanently deported? They asked me to sign the decree. I refused. I told them that I had a job, that my wife was expecting a child, and that there was no justification for my deportation. They replied that they had no say in the matter: the decree had already been sent by Colonel Chakŭrov at the Interior Ministry, who specialized in these matters. Since I still refused to sign, I was told that it hardly mattered, since the order remained valid. All they needed was the signature of two witnesses, and even bureaucrats would do. . . .

I was taken down to the basement and locked in one of the cells I had come to know so well. Inside, there were about fifteen other candidates for deportation. They all seemed to be intelligent people. I remember the name of just one, Pavel Christov. All the others were apparently informed that they would be deported, for they had brought along valises.

We were piled into the back of a jeep, and after making the round of police stations in order to pick up others, we drove to the guardhouse at the central train station. We spent the night there, and the next day were loaded onto a train headed for Ruse. We were accompanied by armed guards.

We nearly died of suffocation in the train wagon because all the windows were closed. At the station in Ruse, we were handed over to other guards and transferred into a truck. We started down the road to Silistra. One of the adjutants proved to be a decent fellow and told us that we were being taken to the Yanko Zabunov cooperative, located in the village of Nozharevo. We spent the night in a detention cell at the Tutrakan police station.

The next day we arrived at our new home, where we were welcomed by the cooperative's director. He told us that there was only farm work to be done, and that we might as well reconcile ourselves to it. He added that the one easy job at the cooperative had already been taken by him. We were given beds at the hostel for young workers and were allowed to take our meals at the cooperative cafeteria. We had to sign in every day at the local police station. We started digging an irrigation canal and worked in the corn and hay fields.

At first, the local villagers looked at us suspiciously. However, once they came to know us better, they began to sympathize with our lot.

My wife gave birth to a boy, and I was given a five-day pass to visit them. At the end of the five days, I went to Colonel Chakŭrov's office at the Ministry of the Interior, on a square near Lion's Bridge,[1] to ask for an additional three days of leave. It was painful to behold the waiting room to Chakŭrov's office. The parents of deportees, having come from all over Bulgaria, were crying and pleading to be seen by this great lord. Their pleas were in vain. Such cruelty, I told myself, could only be the work of someone who was morally or physically handicapped. And, as it turned out, Chakŭrov limped! Although my father was ill, Chakŭrov refused to grant my request for three additional days of leave, and threatened to send me back under armed escort. This evil man had not changed since the days of Lovech. He's the evil genius who destroyed my youth and ruined my life.

At the start of 1965, I was summoned to report for my national service at Botunets. There, too, I was watched relentlessly. Although I had the right to receive and send letters, I was never given the telegram that announced the death of my little boy. I learned the news later, and could not attend the burial. I was certain that they had deliberately withheld the news to avoid granting me the required leave. I completed my term of service without giving them cause to complain. In fact, I was rewarded more than once for my good work. The "school" of Lovech had left its mark.

I returned to Sofia in the hope that I'd finally be forgotten by the authorities—that is, until one fine day when I had a rendezvous with my wife in the park by the city baths. On my way there, I

---

1. A well-known intersection in Sofia, where the headquarters for State Security was located.

bumped into Colonel Chakŭrov. He asked me where I'd been hiding myself. I told him that I'd completed my civil service. Imagine my surprise when the colonel replied that this was not a valid reason to have left Nozharevo. Unmoved by my wife's tears, he told me to follow him to his office, where he wrote a letter ordering me back to Nozharevo. He asked my wife to leave the office, after having advised her to divorce me. Party members, she was told, mustn't spend their lives with the sort of people who had first been sent to camp, then permanently deported from Sofia.

While we were in the middle of this discussion, Gogov, the former head of the camps at Belene and Lovech, walked into the office. He was in street clothes, and I knew that he had retired. Yet it was clear that he still was Chakŭrov's subordinate, for he obeyed the order to take me to the guard station. On our way there, Gogov warned me that I had better not try to escape, since the consequences would be terrible. According to a recent law, those individuals who, without authorization, left the place to which they had been banished would be imprisoned.

And so, I was back in Nozharevo. The village's population was entirely Turk. They were a kind and warmhearted people. Thanks to their compassion, I managed to live well enough until 1978. Apart, that is, from eight months I spent in prison for having left the village without permission. I had gone to Sofia to see my father, who was very sick.

After the six-year deportation, I returned to Sofia. This time, the long arm of Colonel Chakŭrov could not reach me. And, knock on wood, I haven't had any run-ins with the police since then.... But I have been alone since then, too, without family and friends ... just with my memories and nightmares.

NIKOLAS DAFINOV

On 10 March 1962 I received a summons to begin my national service at a factory in Kremikovtsi. The summons arrived "by chance" just a few days after my liberation from Lovech. I was assigned to a work battalion that was 95 percent Gypsy and Turk. We were to build Bulgaria's national treasure: Kremikovtsi.[2] One would have thought that no one cared how this "factory of the future" was being built. With three teams rotating around the clock, we worked day and night. Still, after Lovech, it seemed like a Boy Scouts outing. Twenty days later, and once again "by chance," I was called before the section foreman, Captain Zdravkov, who also represented the Bureau of State Security at the construction site. He warned me to watch my step, for he knew I'd done time at Lovech. I now understood that these were not at all "chance" events. I was in the hot seat, and my every step was being scrutinized. The foreman's shadow was cast over this entire period of my life. I worked at the cement mixer, laying the foundation of the central building at the complex. By an odd slipup, since I had never been a member of a Communist youth organization, I was named Komsomol secretary. But I didn't have the opportunity to pursue my political career. This comic situation in which I found myself—this time truly by chance—was ended by my foreman when he learned what had happened.

I finished my national service. I'd done my part in the building of Kremikovtsi. Finally, the free life that I had so longed for now arrived. I was freed in the spring of 1964. But my joy was short-lived. Barely two weeks later, the Bureau of State Security summoned me to Police Station No. 6. Two officers, by the names of Zandov and Piskov, were waiting there. After having referred to my past, specifically Lovech, they asked me what I now intended to do. I was warned that I had better find a job fast. I replied that I was looking for construction work.

I knew that Mircho Spasov, the man most responsible for the unheard-of horrors that I had survived, was still at Interior. His shadow remained over the life of a former prisoner he had failed to kill at Lovech.

What did I do? I knew no one who could help me. For lack of opportunities to practice, I began to forget the languages I had so wanted to use. Still, in early May I applied for a position with

2. A massive steel-making plant near Sofia that turned out to be an economic and ecological disaster.

Balkantourist.[3] I was overjoyed to learn that I could work at the health resort on the Sun Coast[4] upon presenting myself to a special commission to test my linguistic abilities. On the appointed day, I came before the commission and passed the exam that tested my knowledge of two languages. I received the official appointment and left for the Sun Coast. I hadn't been to the sea since my childhood. I was accompanied to the train station by my mother, who was overjoyed. I settled in at a hostel and assumed my responsibilities at the information office. I was happy and keen to work. The office director, Bayraktarov (from Burgas), was more than satisfied with me. Alas, this period was so short! A month later, a devil in civilian clothes turned up among the foreign visitors with whom I was dealing. He came up to me, muttered my first and last names, and ordered me to follow him to the local police station for an identification check. Once there, a man from the Bureau of State Security battered me with questions. "What are you doing here? Who sent you here?" He ordered me to leave the Sun Coast within four hours if I didn't want to leave under police escort.

I returned to Sofia and worked as a hand compositor, then with a printing firm that produced postage stamps. I was summoned several times for "identification checks," and was banned from a good number of activities. I had to swear that I would go to neither the sea nor the mountains.[5] I also had to swear that I would stay home during the New Year festivities. But I'd never been charged with a crime and swore to myself that I wouldn't fall into their hands. Each time the doorbell rang, my family was paralyzed. My mother suffered from constant anxiety. I was a target for all of the informers and bootlickers thrown up by our Communist prosperity: the Patriotic Front, the Battalion of Volunteers, the Resistance Fighters Against Fascism and Capitalism, the local building officials, and so forth. . . .

I heard that many of those who had survived Lovech were deported immediately after their liberation to isolated regions of the

3. The national tourism office of Bulgaria.
4. A modern vacation complex on the Black Sea, near Nessebar.
5. One risks meeting tourists at vacation sites.

country. At the same time, I learned that Mircho Spasov had been decorated as a "Hero of Socialist Labor."[6] As for the eternal Delcho Chakŭrov, he remained director of the Deportation Service. The service housed Section 5410 of the Bureau of State Security, which had overlapping responsibilities and was run by Colonel Kovachev and his underlings. They outdid one another to accomplish their duty to purge, purge, and purge yet again the nation of criminals and enemies. My turn was next.

One morning I was woken by the doorbell and the all-too-familiar pounding at the door. I was taken to the police station for an "identification check," where the director of the Bureau of State Security charged me under ministerial decree 189, delivered on 23 July 1966. I was deported to the cooperative of Vrani Kon, in the department of Tŭrgovishte.

The road to Tŭrgovishte was lined with the familiar guard-houses. In the trains and stations, people looked in amazement at their fellow traveler wearing handcuffs. At police headquarters in Tŭrgovishte, I was welcomed by Colonel Syarov from the Bureau of State Security. He told me that I would have to report to Colonel Kovachev in Shumen. He described the village I was being sent to, and warned me that any attempt to leave the area would lead to the charge of vagrancy. I was to start work immediately. He called ahead to the cooperative's director, telling him that I would show up for work in a couple of hours.

Forty kilometers outside Omurtag, near the Vŭrbitsa gorge and just five kilometers from the village of the same name, formed by a collection of four neighboring hamlets, was the Turkish village of Vrani Kon. The road from Omurtag to the village was made of gravel and pitted with holes. The area looked like a Mexican canyon. When I stepped out of the bus, having traveled for two hours, past a couple of Turkish villages, I was won over by State Security's genius for finding places of exile. The post office, which happened to be the town's center, was located on a prairie. It was a brick

6. The highest of distinctions for workers, and one that entails material benefits.

one-story building. There were Turks working inside. Across from it was a two-story building that served as the medical center. I continued on my way till I reached the cooperative, which was about a kilometer away from the post office. I came to a gate that blocked the road. It was as if the world ended here, at this gate.

There was a courtyard, a sheep pen, stables, and two or three abandoned cars. In the middle stood an administrative building with sleeping quarters on the first floor for the mechanics. I was assigned a bed in a large room that slept ten. I was usually the only one in the room, unless one of the other workers was kept late and stayed the night. A normal life was hardly possible. The Turks returned to their homes in the hamlets after work. I was usually all alone in the sleeping quarters. My work was loading trucks.

Despite all of my misfortunes, I was lucky on one score: I lived among the Turks. They sympathized and helped me; I think they liked me. The surrounding towns were filled with natives of Sofia. Dozens of families that had been broken thanks to the work of ID (Internment and Deportation). All that I could do was be careful not to make any mistakes that would attract attention. I wanted to avoid being considered a criminal and sent to prison, and so did my best to follow orders to the letter.

One day, while leaving the public baths in Vŭrbitsa (there weren't any in our village), I bumped into Colonel Syarov. He shouted that I was too far from my assigned residence and that this could be seen as an attempt to escape. I began sending appeals every day to Sofia, Shumen, and Tŭrgovishte. I wanted—or, more precisely, I asked—to be transferred to a place where the living conditions were more tolerable. Without result. As for my parents, they prayed for their prodigal son.

A harsh winter arrived. There was almost no work. I thank the Turks once again for their goodness, opening their homes to me so that I wouldn't die of hunger. At the end of 1967, Kovachev took pity on me and transferred me to Popovo, where I worked in felling trees. After the several appeals I had made, this was a sign of favor on his part. I slept at the work sites and was promised that my liberation would follow the World Youth Festival that would take place in Sofia that summer.

August 1968 arrived. I'd been told that my deportation decree was good for three years. I hadn't returned to Sofia during all this time, which was just as well, since I had no desire to see my tormenters.

My respite was short-lived. The nearness of my family, the renewed contact with relatives and friends who had long thought I was dead, brought me back to life. Many people didn't know that I was still alive. But I cannot say the same for those I wish would've forgotten me. A few days after my return to Sofia, I had to change my old identity card, which was covered with red ink and official stamps. As with the Jews, I too carried a mark, but on my identity card. "DEPORTED" was stamped on it several times in big letters. For all I know, the provincial officials considered me potentially dangerous.

After my short visit to Sofia, I once again felt their shadow pass over me. I wondered confusedly how I should live in order to escape them, what sort of work I could do in order to hide from their gaze. I'd worked in construction, as a train station porter, in a cigarette factory, and finally as a telephone technician. I didn't dare think of using my knowledge of foreign languages. In the 1970s, there was an increasing amount of foreign exchange; tourism began to develop; and a number of my friends went abroad, some of them in order to study. But I couldn't even get a simple pass. My mother suffered, sensing that my future was ruined. My father dreamed of my returning to school, but it was too late. I constantly received summons for identity checks from the local and central police stations. I felt that I was always being watched.

Article 14 of the Statutes of the National Police was then in force[7]—in other words, obligatory deportation without the right to be heard or be defended in court. Delcho Chakŭrov was still the president of the commission in charge of deportations.

At the end of October 1972, I was unable to go to work one morning. Though I sent a telegram to my employer four days later

---

7. Modified since 1956, Article 14 empowered the police to intern or deport, without the judgment of the courts, any person they considered socially or politically dangerous.

to say that I was unable to come to work for reasons beyond my control, disciplinary action was taken and I was fired. The reason for my absence was that I'd been held for an identity check at Police Station No. 6. I was put in a cell, and the next day was given bread before being taken to the guardhouse at the train station. I refused to go along this time and wouldn't leave my cell until I was told where I was being sent. The station chief could barely restrain himself, and in a shower of insults shouted that he had received an order from central headquarters to deport me. He read to me Decree No. 1246/72, stipulating that I was to be deported to the village of Svetlene, which was also located in the department of Tŭrgovishte. Once again, Article 14 of the police statutes was cited. It was signed "General Minev."

I was brought before Colonel Syarov, an old acquaintance from Tŭrgovishte. "What do these people want from you, Nikolas? Why have you been sent back?"

These were his very words. Having read the letter that accompanied me, a letter that had been sealed with red wax, he smiled. He told me to leave for my new residence and be careful. I also had to present myself to Colonel Nedev, the chief of police at Popovo.

After I registered at city hall, my destiny was tied to that of the village of Svetlene. For an entire week, no one would rent a room to a deportee from Sofia. People were afraid. With the help of the mayor, I settled down in the home of Old Mavri, who was eighty years old. He rented me two empty rooms coated with bare earth, which I turned into more or less normal living quarters. I began to work as a tile layer at the library they were then building in the center of town. Thanks to my work, I could repress the grim thoughts then turning over in my mind.

Something disagreeable happened to me one day. The prefect of Tŭrgovishte and the regional director of State Security, Traykov and Syarov, were accused of accepting bribes from the Turks who were then being deported. They were removed from their posts. I was disappointed in my "mentors."

After the stint at the library, I worked in a canning plant. I sterilized the entire production line and worked a double shift until midnight. During the official campaign against the Turks, there was no one left to work except the brigades. As a result, I was put in charge of production.[8] I'd provide only quality merchandise, which made me much appreciated.

I couldn't leave the village. I checked in at the police station three times a day. After three police reports stating that I had gone as far as Popovo, which was four kilometers from Svetlene—twice in order to pick up my sheets at the laundry and once to meet my sister at the train station—I was charged with violation of Article 272. In short, vagrancy. In court, when three policemen testified that they had seen me loitering, I had to ask myself if I was dreaming. . . .

The court delivered its sentence: one quarter of my salary would be garnished for eight months, and the sentence would be announced over the village's public address system. It was precisely at this moment that many of the villagers began to sympathize with and help me. I remain good friends with these people, and thank them with all my heart.

I worked for three years in the canning factory. One day in November 1975, a telegram with terrible news arrived: my mother was dying at Pirogov Hospital.[9] I didn't have a moment to spare, and nothing in the world would prevent me from going to her bedside.

She had already died by the time I arrived at the hospital. The unfortunate woman could no longer support the vile abuse that had been piled upon the family because of me.

I was AWOL, and so after the burial I reported to Police Station No. 6. I was allowed to remain an extra two days in Sofia, then had to return to Svetlene.

When I returned, I wrote a petition to be sent to the Central Political Committee, appealing for authorization to return to Sofia. Many of the villagers signed it, and I would like to emphasize once again that the villagers have remained among the best of my friends. Their sheer humanity and willingness to help me bordered on the

8. In order to replace the Turks who had emigrated or been deported or imprisoned, "volunteer" brigades were sent to the villages, composed essentially of grade school and high school students on their summer vacations.

9. An emergency hospital in Sofia.

saintly. To this very day, when I am passing through their region, I stop to visit. They may not have fully understood what was going on, but they were honest and good and sensed the injustice of it all. The further man is from the exercise of power, the more human and decent he is. Thank you, my friends in Svetlene.

Following the signing of the Helsinki Accords in 1976, Article 14 of the Ministry of the Interior was repealed. I was able to return to Sofia. Or, rather, it was my battered body and my soiled, deadened soul that came back.

When I wrote these preceding pages, I stirred up the terrible memories of the Communist butchery that had for so many years jolted me awake in the middle of the night. Why revive, I asked myself, memories of the barbarians from State Security and the Political Bureau? Why bring back the nightmare of the long years in camp and exile? But I knew the answer. This must never again happen! Never! Not under any pretext whatsoever! The Communists like to say that nothing and no one is forgotten. Wouldn't it then be the height of cynicism to forget their victims from Belene, Lovech, Skravena, and so forth? To forget the genocide carried out with extraordinary and thoroughly Eastern cruelty against the fine flower of our society? May God be my witness: it was easier to overcome my fear of the revenge of the State Security apparatus than my disgust for those murderers who until recently controlled the most important levers of power. A new and unprecedented Christian mass must be said for all the martyrs of the Communist concentration camps. But this must be preceded by broadcasting the truth, all the truth and nothing but the truth. Regardless of the price we, the former "dregs" of the People's Republic of Bulgaria, paid for the truth, we must suppress our fear on behalf of our contemporaries as well as the future generations and cry out: "Only God knows that we survived by sheer luck! Still, our duty is to demand an explanation from these assassins who killed hundreds of innocent victims! Who mutilated, humiliated, buried alive thousands of saints in their Communist paradise!" It's thus that we'll free ourselves from our fear and that God, in his infinite mercy, will save our Christian souls.

BOZHIDAR PETROV

I cannot express the joy I felt. But it lasted only a short time: a few hours after my liberation, I learned that my entire family had been deported to a village more than four hundred kilometers from Sofia. Our house had been taken over by a director of the headquarters of the National Police. We had lived there for ten years. It was Colonel Chakŭrov who was then in charge of deportations. The same man who, in the company of General Mircho Spasov, came to inspect the camp. We went to plead with him at his office in the headquarters of State Security at the Lions' Bridge. He was a very powerful man. He waved letters we'd written to the minister, to the government, and to Chakŭrov himself. Laughing, he asked, "You haven't yet understood that I am the one who decides everything?"

The waiting room was filled with people from all over Bulgaria who were as unfortunate and powerless as we were. Chakŭrov passed by in review, limping slightly, and dismissed half of us with the words, "Do you have an authorization? No? Then get out of here before I order a police escort to take you back!"

And the people would leave in tears. Traveling under police escort was not fun. It took six days to reach Varna,[10] but I was taken off the train on the fifth day, when we reached Shumen. Back then, the city was known as Kolarovgrad. I was still handcuffed, being a "potentially dangerous case." The handcuffs were taken off only when I slept in the series of relay stations. The guards were changed at each station; each had its own transportation police, which is why the trip took so long. In fact, the policemen at the guardhouses remembered me from the previous trips I had made. I arrived at about five o'clock in the morning at Shumen. I was taken to the police chief. He was a colonel whose name I've forgotten but who treated me decently. He even said several times, "Stay here with us, young man. The people back in Sofia are going to ruin your health."

In 1963 the actor Vladimir Trendafilov rallied to our cause, as did the writer Dimitûr Simidov, the singer Magda Pushkarova,

---

10. Varna is on the Black Sea, about four hundred kilometers from Sofia.

and other well-known artists. The minister canceled our deportation orders and restored our rights. But Chakŭrov renewed the official decree and read it out to us, along with a second one that forbade us to return to our house.

"If you agree with the statement, sign at the bottom of the sheet." But my father told me to sign nothing, and I of course obeyed him. Chakŭrov placed in front of us the ministerial decree on which our names were written, and crossed out both my brother's name and mine. He clearly held our fate in his hands. Once again, I was handcuffed and led from guardhouse to guardhouse. I remember that, on one occasion, the handcuffs were too tight, and I asked my guard to loosen them. He looked down at the envelope sealed in red wax and said, "But you're especially dangerous. If you go on talking, I'll make the cuffs even tighter."

My hands hadn't fully recovered from camp, and I thought that my wrists were going to break. I asked once again for the cuffs to be loosened. The guard pointed his machine gun at me and shouted, "One more word and I'll shoot!"

There were other individuals in the train car who'd been arrested. I hit the window with my cuffs and broke it. The guards ran to the car and started to beat me. But then one of them opened the letter and said, "Leave him alone. He isn't under arrest, but is being deported."

After ten years had passed, the colonel finally granted us our house, and my family was again back together. I was already married and had a son. My brother said he could no longer live in Bulgaria. At the very moment our house was returned to us, he fled to West Germany. He has since married and has two children. He's now fifty-two years old. During the ten years that passed after his escape, various bureaucrats repeatedly summoned me to the Interior Ministry to remind me that my brother was a traitor to his fatherland.

Thanks to Article 14, thousands of Bulgarians were deported without trial or sentencing. This was entirely the work of Colonel Chakŭrov. Our passports were officially stamped, on the page that carried our address, with the word "DEPORTED." We could only work in the place where we were assigned. In the villages, abandoned houses were rented to us. We had to register everyday at the mayor's office. We were initially looked upon with suspicion by the locals. Public opinion was, in various ways, deliberately and systematically manipulated, portraying the camp prisoners as especially dangerous criminals. But their suspicions gradually disappeared, and they taught us how to work in the fields and helped us.

Our schedule was divided into "workdays," and we were paid at the end of the year. In the agricultural brigades, we earned up to a lev each day. The locals were able to live, since they had livestock and a small plot of land they could cultivate on their own. There was no work during winter. Those who had their own means lived well enough, but for those of us who could only count on our hands and backs, we couldn't eat or pay our rent. During these difficult periods, the locals gave us a hand. In general, the deported families were forced to sign a declaration in which they turned over their houses to the state. As for those who didn't have homes, they were told by Chakŭrov to stay where they had been sent, under the pretext that there was no available housing in either the cities or their native provinces. Police bureaucrats with their families moved into what had been our own homes. They paid us a standard monthly rent of five to ten leva, and we were forbidden, according to the law, from either lodging a complaint or demanding the return of our property.

There were yet others who were deported individually. The families remained in their native provinces, while the deportees had to seek permission to visit their fathers and mothers, brothers and sisters. Chakŭrov's power was that great. He divided up and relocated families, deported and assigned individuals to house arrest. The fate of tens of thousands of Bulgarians was in his hands. He reassured us by asking that we hold on for a few more years. Once we earned the right, we would be allowed to return to our homes. Yet to others, he said that they would never again see their homes. Every appeal, every complaint addressed to various bureaus, passed through his hands.

The local officials of the Interior Ministry had the right to authorize deportees to leave their assigned residences for a few days. However, one needed a good reason: a serious illness in the family, a death, or the like. We traveled with administrative passes upon which we depended entirely. Everywhere we went we ran into a vast bureaucratic structure whose doors closed for the most minor of reasons.

For years I have read and reread all that has been written on state repression and inquisitions. The camps in French Guyana (described by René Belbénoit),[11] Hitler and Stalin, Geshev, and Fereshtanov[12] do not compare to the bureaucrats at the Bureau of State Security and the Interior Ministry during this period—I mean the era of beatings and mass murder. But don't forget that there remained isolated cases up to 10 November 1989.

All of this is now history. Our lives are behind us now, and unfortunately we have no other memories.

11. Belbénoit is the author of a work published in France and titled *Les compagnons de la belle* (Paris, 1939).

12. The men responsible for the measures of repression in Bulgaria before 9 September 1944.

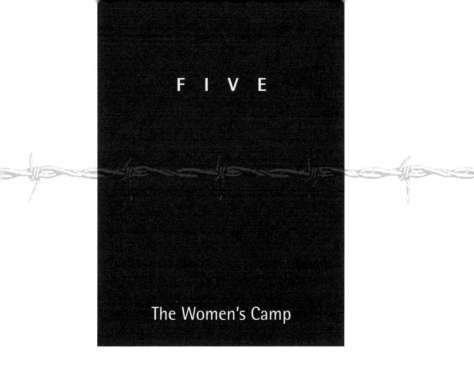

F I V E

The Women's Camp

LILYANA PIRINCHEVA

I am a pharmacist by training and was thirty years old when I found myself in one of the camps.[1] I was released nearly six years later, having been at both Belene and Bosna. When I think about all that can be said regarding the awful conditions, the truly awful conditions at these camps.... At Bosna, we actually lived in a stable. We worked like beasts of burden in the fields. We were constantly humiliated, and the clothes we were given were no less humiliating: they were old, tattered army fatigues. We worked from morning to night, under the blazing sun of summer and in the paralyzing cold of winter.

1. This section is extracted from *The Survivors*.

By far the worst thing, though, was what happened to our souls. In the camps where I was imprisoned, the prisoners didn't die and weren't killed. Those who became seriously ill were in fact sent away so that they wouldn't die in the camp. The horror of these camps was that they turned thousands of people into human wrecks. It was as if our hearts had been extinguished or ruined. Ruined by the humiliations, the hard and often absurd labor. Our work was like Sisyphus's pushing of the rock: it sapped our moral and psychological strength, our dignity, and our integrity. The Sisyphean nature of work also existed at Bosna. In the autumn, for example ... we were taken to the fields. Arranged in long rows, we spent the entire day breaking lumps of dried soil with the backs of our hoes.

We survived, however, because we kept our humanity—and did so despite their best effort to persuade us, day in, day out, and around the clock, that we were useless, that we were vermin and a danger to society. They humiliated us and tried to sap our ability to think for ourselves. In our ranks were anarchists, Trotskyites, Agrarians, and those who refused all labels and party affiliations. In this intolerable atmosphere of daily hardship and hard and pointless labor, we were saved by that aspiration shared by all human beings—namely, the desire for dignity, humanity, and goodness.

Let me tell you a story. One day we were working at the dike. The work was extremely hard. A bird of prey suddenly passed not too far above us, carrying an animal of some sort in its beak. We shouted, and the bird took fright and dropped its prey. Into our midst fell what turned out to be a young rooster. We picked it up and could have eaten it on the spot, we were all so hungry. But instead, we kept the rooster. He symbolized man's ability to escape from the jaws of death. We spoiled the rooster, and he became a real character, standing in front of us during morning and evening lineups. We all loved that rooster. He became our good-luck charm, our talisman. And then, one day, he disappeared. We were all worried and looked for him high and low. Finally, we understood what had happened. A new group of women had arrived the night before. There was a Gypsy among them, who had already been sent to the camp one or two times. Her name was Gina, and we were sure she was the thief. We surrounded her and asked what she had done with the rooster. Gina began to cry and said that she had broken the bird's neck in order to eat him. We forced her to give him back to us. We dug a small grave and buried him in it. We were all heartbroken, but though we were also starving, we didn't dare eat him.

This isn't the only example of the power of the human spirit.... For example, we all agreed that whenever a package arrived, we would give it to whomever was ill. Though starving, we wouldn't allow ourselves to eat a single thing from the package. It was for our sick comrade.

I can draw certain conclusions from all of this. The camps were not only a place of physical destruction and mutilation (for all of us, without exception, left the camps mutilated to one degree or another). They were also places where the individual's moral character and dignity were undermined. We were incessantly told that we were the scum of society and that we had to be eliminated. Many of us could not withstand both the awful physical conditions, which pushed our bodies and nerves to the breaking point, and the moral torture. There was the combination of miserable material conditions, hard and pointless labor that resembled Sisyphus's boulder, unrelenting brainwashing, the stream of total disinformation, separation from one's home, and the constant reminders that the fate of our families was in our hands. All of this turned the camp inmates into an amorphous mass, into people who had given up completely, or others who became undercover agents, or informants. In other words, into anything that the authorities wanted to turn us into.

PETRUNKA BONEVA

In 1947–48 I was imprisoned in the camp at Bosna, which was near the men's concentration camp in Nozharevo.[2] I was sent there because I was guilty of having had a romantic liaison with a resident foreigner (I was seeing the French consul to Bulgaria back then,

2. This section was published in *Demokratsia*, 23 April 1990.

Réginald de Varenne). He had asked me to marry him, but I refused because I wouldn't leave my mother.

We weren't beaten at Bosna. On the other hand, many of our precious and personal belongings were taken from us and never returned.

Once I was liberated, I returned to Sofia, even though I was born in a village in the region of Samokov. I was often summoned to various police stations, where I was forced to sign statements that I was collaborating with the authorities. I had no choice but to sign, since they used force. I don't remember the names of my inquisitors, but there were a few. There was one who was slightly more human than the others. He forced me to cry out loud so that his colleagues would think that he was beating me. But even though I signed these statements, I never collaborated with the police. It isn't my nature to do such a thing.

In 1951, I got married and then very quickly divorced, even though I continued to live with my ex-husband. We had property in a suburb of Sofia (which is where my house is now located), and we wanted to build a house on it. Yet we had a number of problems with our neighbor, whose brother worked at the Ministry of the Interior. He was the one responsible for arranging my imprisonment at Belene in 1958.

I was held at Belene for about one and a half months, after which rumors began to circulate that the camp would be closed. It was then that they took thirteen women, including myself, and about fifty men and brought us to the rock quarries at Lovech. The women were put into a chicken coop, since there was no other place for us. It was only later that we were given other quarters. There were only a few of us at first, which meant that we were beaten that much more. Once there were more than one hundred women prisoners, the beatings were no longer as systematic. The name of one of the guards was Yulia; another was called Totka; and a third, whose name I can no longer recall, was the most brutal. Soon thereafter, a fourth female guard arrived.

I recall Majors Gogov and Goranov, who both lived in the camp. They didn't sleep with the inmates. We were too horrible to look at. Broken by work beyond our strength, dressed in old army fatigues, coated with blood . . . we couldn't have been very attractive. Along with their female counterparts, however, Gogov and Goranov beat us. They used grooved clubs, which hurt horribly.

Certain prisoners were picked from our ranks to serve as brigade chiefs, and they also beat us. But among the women there were fewer deaths from beatings than there were among the men. Though our guards hit us, they didn't try to kill us. Still, accidents happened. I remember one small and frail woman from Knyazhevo who told us that she'd recently divorced her husband, who was a policeman. They had a child who was nine years old. Following the divorce, she had won a state housing lottery and had been given a two-room apartment. Her ex-husband had had her imprisoned in the camp in order to become the child's guardian and take possession of the apartment. The poor woman died after her very first beating.

We worked until noon on Sundays, after which we were taken to the baths. When we returned from the work site, each of us had to carry a large stone while our police escort formed a sort of gauntlet and lashed out with long pipes. It was almost more than we could stand.

After my liberation in 1960, I was deported to my native village. While I was traveling to Samokov one day, I discovered that the fellow sitting next to me was a deputy from Sofia. He was the one who told me about the role played by the United Nations in the closing of the camp.[3]

There is something else that I need to say. Soon after I was sent to Belene, they came for my brother, who was still living in our hometown, and took him to the police station. He was kept there for a couple of days and beaten almost nonstop so that he'd sign a paper affirming that his sister had wanted to flee the country. But he never signed it. No one related in one way or another to camp inmates was spared. . . .

---

3. In the wake of stories in the Western media, the question of the camps was raised in the United Nations. This is probably one of the reasons for the temporary and partial closing of the camps.

NADYA DUNKIN

I was an actress at the National Theater in Plovdiv. My father was an engineer, and my mother was the daughter of a Greek Orthodox priest. Although my parents were well-off, they taught me the importance of work. And I enjoyed working. After I finished my schooling, I entered the theater at Plovdiv. One day we were rehearsing a play that contained outrageous Communist propaganda. I refused to go along with it. To my way of seeing, the teaching of Christ was truer than that of Communism. I made no secret of my beliefs, but did so at a time when Bulgaria was swarming with informers (people who really wanted to win the regime's favor) who were using the Communist Party for personal gain. I was eventually denounced.

Early one morning in 1959, someone rang at our door. I assumed it was someone checking our address, which was fairly common at the time. I opened the door and saw two policeman and a plainclothesman. "Would you get dressed and come with us to the police station for an address check?" "Yes," I answered without asking any questions.

I wasn't really worried. I didn't have a police record; I'd never harmed anyone and had nothing to fear. I quickly got dressed and stepped outside, where an official car was waiting. The window curtains were drawn so that no one could see inside. I got in and was taken to the police station. I was led into a kind of basement, where I was kept for three, maybe four hours. A door finally opened, and a policeman I hadn't seen before asked me to accompany him. I thought I was being freed. But to my surprise, I was put into a car and driven to the guardhouse at the train station. Not one of the guards said a word during this entire time. While I was waiting at the guardhouse, another woman was brought in. She was in tears and kept crying out, "My little baby, my little baby!"

"Why are you crying?" I asked.

We didn't know one another, but she took me in her arms and said, "I was arrested because I saw my husband with his mistress near the marketplace. I was shocked, ran up to him, and tore off his officer stripes. He's in the military, you see. And we've a two-year-old child. He told me that he was going to get rid of me. Obviously, he'd already arranged for my deportation. It's a bad sign to be in this guardhouse. It means that we're being deported."

Her name was Margarita. This was when there were mass deportations in Bulgaria.

"Even if this is true," I replied, "there are worse things than deportation. We'll be somewhere else; we'll manage to live one way or another. Please don't cry: I've a son, too, but tears won't help us now. We've got to be strong. The important thing is to be healthy."

My own son was seven years old at the time. Margarita and I were alone in the guardroom, which gave us the chance to get to know one another. She told me she was a nurse, and we spoke of many things. We wondered about what was going to happen and why we were there, but didn't have any answers. We spent the night in the guardroom and were given nothing to eat or drink. Early the next morning the door to the room opened and a policeman barked, "Get dressed immediately. There are men waiting outside, but do not talk to them."

We got ready and walked into the courtyard. The men all seemed to be in a state of shock and pain; many of them also seemed to be cultured and intelligent. Glancing at the hands of one of them standing near me, I noticed that his nails had not been cut in months. He approached me while a policeman was looking elsewhere and whispered, "Be brave! Don't let them break you!"

We started out. The men were the first to be taken to the train station, followed by the women. Before we were separated for good at the station, the same man again managed to approach me. "I'm a former officer. Don't let them break you." It was the second time he said this to me, and he also handed me a flask. At that very moment, the policeman came running up and screamed, "What has he given you?"

"A flask," I answered. "For water. I haven't had any water to drink since yesterday afternoon."

He let me keep the flask. We were then loaded into a rail car and put into a compartment that was guarded by three policemen. I asked if they knew that neither we nor our families knew where we were being taken. I asked them if they knew where we were going. I asked them if they knew why were we there. But the only answer I got was, "You'll see." It was said in so coarse and repulsive a tone that I didn't dare ask any more questions. The silence lasted a few hours, until we reached the station at Pleven, where we were forced to get out and wait in a guardhouse once again. The door opened and a police officer entered. He stood out from the others: he was polite, spoke well, and was very courteous. He even complimented me. My skin back then was very white, and he turned to me and said, "The Sun Coast is too hot for your beautiful white face."[4]

These were his words, but I didn't understand what he meant. He was a handsome man, and perhaps he found me attractive. He asked if we'd like to eat something and told us that we'd be leaving the next day. And he then repeated his remark about the Sun Coast. When he left the room, I turned to my unfortunate companion: "Margarita, this officer is trying to tell us something. He's telling us that we're headed for a terrible place and that we ought to escape."

But how could we have escaped when we were guarded by three policemen? Besides, there was no reason to escape, since I hadn't committed a crime. We were again put on a train. The landscape passed by the window, while Margarita cried softly to herself and I held back my tears. I was still confident that God was all-powerful and that he wouldn't abandon us. I'd been raised as a Christian: after all, wasn't I the granddaughter of a priest? My faith was solid and helped me a great deal. After a few hours on the train, we arrived at Lovech.

Only then did it dawn upon us that we weren't being deported. Instead, we were being sent to a camp about which we had heard rumors. Though its existence wasn't generally known, I had heard vague reports about Lovech. While we were loaded into a truck, passersby tossed us cigarettes and chocolate bars. They seemed to take pity on us. But our guards forbade us to pick up these

---

4. The Sun Coast is the name of a beach resort on the Black Sea, and is here used derisively to refer to the camp at Lovech.

gifts, and we drove off. My first impression was of a somber, nightmarish landscape. We drove through a narrow valley surrounded by towering rocks. After we passed through a tunnel, the truck stopped and we were taken off. A man resembling Quasimodo appeared. He was a Gypsy named Shakho; he was bowlegged and had a repulsive, murderous face. Appropriately enough, he turned out to be a murderer: we learned that he had even killed his own brother in the camp. He walked up to me and started to hit me with a whip. I protected my eyes, terrified that I'd be blinded. It was terrible: he must have hit me twenty times. The pain was too much, and I finally fainted.

He then moved on to Margarita. She began to cry, "My little boy. Jesus Christ, save me! My little boy!" Every time Margarita cried, "My little boy," Shakho hit her even harder. He finally stopped. The two of us were sprawled on the ground. Looking up, we saw crows hovering and cawing above the rocks. It seemed like so great a space, surrounded by cliffs on all sides. How could one escape from such a place? Even the birds couldn't fly above the walls of stone. We eventually found ourselves in a sort of underground shelter filled with rows of three-tiered wooden beds. Margarita and I were frightened and didn't say a word at first. Then I told her, "Margarita, God will help us. Yes, it's really horrible. We're in a concentration camp. We'll need all our strength to fight against this hell."

We were allowed to wash ourselves; then we waited. A half hour passed, and a gray battalion appeared, called the death battalion. Wounded and crippled men, covered with bandages, their faces swollen by untreated toothaches. As they walked past us, it seemed that they were intellectuals. Draped in long coats that partly hid their rags, wearing shoes riddled with holes, they were exhausted and could barely drag themselves along. I cried out, "Look, Margarita: it's the gray battalion!" The women then followed. They all seemed to be bright and perceptive. They hugged us upon arriving and flooded us with questions: "Where have you come from? Does the outside world know about us and this camp? Have you any money? Cigarettes?"

It so happened that I always carried some money in my bag. There was a store of sorts in the camp, and I told the women, "Here, take my money. I don't smoke, but I know what it's like to be a smoker." Perhaps it was the money. But whatever the reason, the women took to me.

The next day we were lined up. A voice called out, "The actress! Step forward!" I found myself standing in front of a policewoman I'd never before seen in my life. Pretty and well built, she walked up to me. "And so, you're the actress? Do you remember the theater in Plovdiv? I do. I was an actress there, too. But you were a snob who paid no attention to me, since you were always given the best roles."

"But that's not possible. How could you have been in the theater company without my recognizing you?"

"And so, you don't recognize me?"

With that, she became furious. It was clear that this was all the excuse she wanted to beat me. She began to hit me. The other prisoners closed their eyes, and I gritted my teeth and thought I was going to faint. But I didn't cry out.... All of us prisoners were beaten with whips: look at my fingers and back. They're covered with scars. They hit us in the small of the back, around the kidneys.... When they killed someone, it was with the blade of an axe in the back. This is how they killed the men.

"This is so you'll remember the theater in Plovdiv!" She then shouted, "The other new arrival, step forward!" Margarita stepped up.

"But why do you want to hit me? What have I done? Have I been convicted of a crime? I've a small child. I beg you, please, let me go. Why do you want to kill us?"

Her questions were answered with another question: "Ah, so you want to know what it is you did to me?" And with that, the guard had another excuse to begin beating a prisoner. This guard was known as Beautiful Yulia. She was merciless. Poor Margarita cried and screamed. She couldn't bear the beating—she was too frail. I was better at keeping it all in and never gave them the pleasure of showing them how much I suffered.... This was our "introduction" to life at Lovech.

—

We slept in a stable, where we each had about forty or fifty centimeters of bed space. When one of us turned over to her other side, everybody else had to turn as well. There were no blankets. We slept on straw mattresses and had bricks for pillows. There were about two hundred women. When we assembled at night, we'd ask one another why we were there. Or if we knew who had been behind it. It turned out that none of us had ever been tried or convicted of a crime. Most of us were intellectuals.

—

We were on our way to work in the village of Bŭlgarene. I had never used a pickaxe before in my life. We had to gather the corn in order to help a brigade that was falling short of its quota. It was very hot, and the sky was blazing down on us. I began to dig, and the soil had grown rock-hard from the lack of rain. The veteran prisoners on either side of me said, "They're digging a grave for us, and a grave for you. If you start to lag behind, you'll be whipped." Having said this, they began to help me. I felt weak, and the July sun was blistering. I had a heat stroke and collapsed that first day. Though I don't remember, the other prisoners told me that I was beaten up and thrown into the bushes. If I could withstand the treatment, I'd go on working; if I couldn't, I'd die.

"The actress isn't long for this world."

At one point, while I was lying unconscious on the ground, the most brutal of the guards caught a grass snake and tossed it on top of me. The snake hissed and slithered off into the grass. "She must be dead, since the snake has run off," she said.

The others continued to work. But they also had to take my body, put it in a sack, and either dump it in the Danube or give it to the pigs. They picked me up, and my head rolled from one side to the other. Seeing the foam on my lips and my blank stare, my fellow inmates said, "Ah, the poor one," and started to cry. When we arrived in camp, they tossed me to the dogs and locked the gates. The huge guard dogs were kept tied up. And I was thrown near them, the next morning to be put in a sack and thrown into the river. God, however, had the last word. At that very moment, the men were coming back from work. They passed by, and a doctor who afterward died in the camp (he had been a Party secretary in a Sofia hospital) saw me and took my pulse.

"Her heart is still beating, but barely. In an hour she'll be dead." Since he took care of the camp personnel, he gave me an injection of camphor. And a miracle took place. When I opened my eyes, all I remember was thinking that I was already dead. I was surrounded by the night and stars. I'd regained consciousness before dawn. It must have been around three o'clock in the morning, because soon thereafter the bugle sounded the 3:30 reveille. Yet I was conscious before it sounded. "Where am I?" I asked aloud. It was still dark; I tried to recall what my world had become and where I now found myself. I looked above and saw the stars shining, when suddenly I was overcome by fear. "Give a hand!" The guards had heard me, and picked me up as if I were a sack of potatoes and threw me in the barracks. The other prisoners began screaming, for they all thought that I was dead. The poor women were scared. But the old hands said, "Stop screaming! She has simply revived. Be quiet! She'll recover, and don't scare her. Having survived this, she will not die anytime soon."

They covered me with old rags and left me alone. The next day everyone went to work, while I was locked up for the entire day with no food or water or medication. I was too weak to get up, due to my bruises and all that I had endured the day before. I'd been brutally beaten. I was in a coma for fourteen hours, and survived by a miracle.

﹏

Each day I felt that I was getting closer to death. Everything had been calculated to torture us. It was planned out. We were allowed a single letter every six months. Let's not talk about the food. Even the dogs would never have eaten our daily meals, though it seems that they eat everything. And you mustn't forget our sleeping arrangements, beatings without warning or reason, impossible quotas, ice-cold water in the bathroom during the winter, and so forth. This was camp life.

As for work, we dug up and loaded rocks that weighed thirty, forty, fifty kilos each. They weighed more than we did. We also filled wheelbarrows with soil. We worked in teams of five. When we fell short of our quota, we each were given twenty strokes of the whip. And when the handcart accompanied us to work in the morning, we knew that one of us would be killed during the day. Some of the prisoners, in order to save their own skin, agreed to beat the others. This allowed those who were actually paid to beat the prisoners to rest from time to time. (Kina, for example, and Totka, who came from a village near Pleven. Totka was the most violent of all: she was the one who broke my finger.)

All the women prisoners had professional backgrounds of one sort or another. School bursars, painters, nurses, accountants. I was an actress. At least I had my faith. There were many others who didn't believe in God, yet I'd tell them that it was God alone who would save us from these monsters with human faces.

———

The dogs began to bark like mad one night. We actually thought that the camp was besieged and that others were trying to free us. It was the only thing we thought of. When morning arrived, we saw that there were guards and their dogs all over the valley. A young man, the son of a Party member from Burgas, had escaped. He had knocked down a guard with a blow to the head and lit off. They couldn't find him. It was said that he made his way to the town of Lovech and revealed what was happening in the camp. But we weren't helped by these revelations.

———

There was one guard who was humane. He told us one day, "I can't stand to watch you suffer any longer. I'm turning in my uniform." And he actually resigned, though we tried to convince him to stay. He simply couldn't, for he clearly was at a breaking point. He was nicknamed Little Salamander because, when he guarded us, it always was "raining" and he ordered us indoors. When he came on duty, we'd say to ourselves, "At least today we won't be murdered."

One day, while working in the rock quarry, I was approached by a high-ranking officer. "Were you ever an actress?" he asked. "What roles did you play?"

"Comrade," I answered, "don't ask me what roles I played before. Instead, ask me about the role I am now playing: you see, I am bowing out."

He looked at me with pity and didn't reply. He walked up to a second, a third, then a fourth woman. That same evening I said to the others, "That man will save all of us." And, in fact, when we woke up one morning two or three weeks later, we were told, "The following women whose names are called will not work today." About fifty women were freed that day. The rest of us—we must have been about one hundred—were transferred to the camp at Skravena.[5] We were taken there in a truck, and as we were crossing through Botevgrad, we were ordered to sing. And sing we did. We pretended to be happy; we pretended that we'd never been beaten. Still, our lives had been saved. Who was responsible? We never found out. Was it that handsome man who seemed so elegant and perceptive?

By the time we reached Skravena, however, we were so exhausted and emptied that we seemed condemned to death, if not already half-dead. It was as if all our strength had been sapped, and it was all we could do to drag ourselves from place to place. It was so cold that when returning from the quarry, we gathered cigarette paper, scraps, all sorts of garbage to serve as fuel for a fire. We'd light the fire in the courtyard and try to warm our bluish hands. At Skravena, our emotional well-being was more threatened than our physical health. Day in, day out, we were told, "You're going to die here. Even if you remain alive, you'll never again be a human being. Did you really think that you would escape this place?"

Yet the villagers pitied us. When we walked by the public fountain, we'd sometimes find bread, cheese, butter, and cigarettes that were deliberately left there. But we were severely punished if we

5. In September 1961, the women at Lovech were transferred to Skravena.

were caught trying to talk to the villagers. One woman tried to take a newspaper from a truck driver who was transporting rocks to Botevgrad. She was beaten to death. The world was never to learn about us.[6]

—

Two incidents occurred at Skravena that I'll never forget. Though they happened so long ago, I still remember them. I live with these memories and will never be able to forget them.

While we were working the quarry one day, what should we see? Two men were brought in, a young man and one who was older. We soon learned that they were father and son. The killers arrived moments after the two men had put down their suitcases. The young man was maybe twenty-five, at most twenty-six years old. His father was a well-known painter from Ruse. While he was kept to one side, those sadistic killers, all big and strong, began to beat the man's son under his very eyes.

"Look at your son!" they ordered. But he covered his eyes and could barely remain standing. And we saw them, and they saw us. The rock quarry was like an arena. The poor boy was beaten unconscious. All he was able to cry was, "Daddy, Daddy, they're going to kill me. Help me, save me. They're killing me, they're killing me, Daddy!"

It was unbearable. We were all crying. It was horrible, just horrible! They then turned on the father and beat the life out of him. The boy died the next day, while the father died three days later. This was how our "correctional" system worked: the living daylights were beaten out of you when you arrived. If you survived, you worked. If you didn't, you died.[7]

6. One local farmer, whose house was about a hundred meters from the camp, recounts, "I can't say, I don't remember anything. Maybe they were screaming, maybe they were singing. I didn't see anything, I didn't hear anything, I just can't say" (*Demokratsia*, 27 May 1990). A second local remarks, "We were told they were criminals. And so, we thought little of their treatment. We thought they were getting what they deserved" (*The Survivors*).

7. A male prisoner also witnessed this same incident: "They were brought to the quarry, where Gazdov and Goranov were waiting. And Goranov wanted to force

The second incident that I'll never forget involved a beautiful young woman who was a native of Sofia and a professional accountant. She often spoke about her child. But she finally went too far. One day she said to the guards, "Just wait—your turn will come. You're animals, not men. Go ahead and hit me. I refuse to work. I wasn't made to work in the quarries. Hit me, I want to die."

She was deliberately provoking them. And like the animals they were, they started to hit her. And they forced us to watch as a reminder and lesson. She shouted, "I'm not a criminal. I won't work in the quarry. I want to know why I'm here. I insist upon a trial. How dare you hit me, you murderers!" At that point, they began to beat her mercilessly. But the woman refused to get up and go to work. She wouldn't give in. A guard said, "What are you doing standing around listening to her? Set her hair on fire and let's see if that will persuade her to go to work." And so they set a match to her hair; the flames flew up; suddenly all of her head seemed to be aflame, and they went on beating her until she was unconscious. The sight was too awful to bear, too awful to watch. The woman died in terrible agony. I remember her last words: "My baby, my baby . . . Sofia, Buz . . . " She must have meant Buzludzha Street. But we could not get her last name, which we needed to help us find her family and tell them how she had died—that is, if we survived ourselves to tell the story. One can never forget such things.

Journalists from the BBC recently visited, and we showed them the camp. They took photos, and I showed them the rock nearly a hundred meters high from which men and women would throw themselves when they had reached their breaking point. I was the one who saved the life of Lili Zakhova, the daughter of the well-known judge. She wanted to jump off the top of the rock just three days after she had arrived in the camp. I pulled her from behind,

---

the father to kill his son. He gave him a hammer to hit his son with. The boy screamed, "No!" The father was then forced to hit his son. The boy began to cry, "Daddy, Daddy!" The screaming went on and on, and the women who were at the top of the quarry began to cry. Those of us below turned our backs in order not to see what was happening. This was how they killed this father's child under his eyes" (*The Survivors*).

took her in my arms, and told her, "We mustn't die! We've got to hang on!" My words had an effect, and Lili snapped back to life.

Human beings are remarkably resilient. It was Saint-Exupéry who said that man can bear what no animal possibly can. When I saw myself in the documentary film *The Survivors*, I wondered, "My God, how did I manage to survive?" Dante's *Inferno* cannot begin to compare with our lives in the camps. There aren't words dramatic enough to convey what we experienced. You could only understand if you experienced it yourself.... But to recount the experience is a very different matter. Though the dead cannot speak, the survivors have finally begun to speak.

As for Gogov, Goranov, and the other criminals, not only are they still free, but half of these people haven't given up their Communist ideals. They're still capable of misleading innocent people with these lies. In my opinion, this system is just horrible. It can bring us no good and must never be revived. We must never allow Communism to return. I wouldn't want anyone delivered to our death camp—for that's what it was: a death camp—but it must also be understood that such a place actually existed. And that there must never again be a Communist regime.

When I returned home and rang the doorbell of our apartment, I was so skinny and frail that I must have looked like a corpse. It was my mother who opened the door. She thought she was looking at my ghost and fainted right at my feet. She had suffered so much on my account, and it was too much for her.

Because I was well known in Plovdiv as an actress, the patriarch Kiril himself learned,[8] soon after my liberation, that I had been imprisoned in a camp. It seems that he told his associates to say, should they see me, that I must meet with him. And so, one day I went to his chambers and asked to be announced. "Ah, yes," I was told, "he's been waiting for you and still asks if you have come by to see him." When I was led to him, the patriarch said, "My daughter, my daughter: what did they do to you? Sit down, my daughter, and tell me all that you went through."

8. The head of the Orthodox Church of Bulgaria.

I thus begin to tell my story, and I said to him, "Grandfather (which is the form of address we use for patriarchs), you won't look at me with the eyes of a man. And so, I can show you all my scars. My back will always be scarred from the whippings." I was wearing a light shirt: it was summer and the weather was very warm. I took it off and lowered my skirt a little to show him what had been done to the small of my back. I then turned around to face him: "Look, Grandfather, look at what they did to me!"

He turned away—have you ever seen a patriarch cry?—and asked, "How did you survive, my daughter? You must be a believer."

"Yes," I answered.

"And so, God was at your side."

I showed him my broken fingers, there where . . .

"You will never know peace, my daughter. You will always be their enemy, and they will pursue you to the ends of the earth because you were in the camp. You're too dangerous. They'll always be afraid that you will tell of the horrors you saw. And so, I will put you under my protection. Come back in three days. There is no need to write a letter; simply come directly to the archives office, take a seat at the table, and begin your work. Everything will be arranged."

He was a true Christian. I didn't have to plead for his protection, since he knew all too well the nature of the concentration camps. He saved my life. Most of the others haven't been as fortunate. They cannot find work, for no one will hire them for anything but the most physically demanding of jobs. I spent eight years with the Orthodox Synod. My son has since supported me. Both he and his wife are chemists and live in Hannover. But I was never given the official authorization to visit them. . . . Well, there you have it. I am alive and in good health. I'm grateful for that: after all, many people never left the camp alive.

THE
OTHER
SIDE

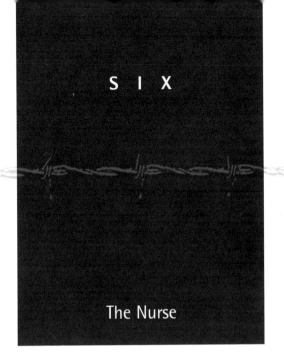

S I X

The Nurse

GEORGI IOSIFOV

I'm a former inmate of the camps at Nozharevo, Belene, Lovech, where I was known as Zhoro of Varna. . . .[1] Even now there are very few people willing to talk about their experiences in the camps. They're still afraid! I am, too. Yes, I'm afraid, but my sons are now grown up and can fend for themselves. So why should I be afraid? Because the gun is still loaded and in the hands of old men — seventy, eighty years old — who won't hesitate to fire. I know that if the Communists returned to power, they could reopen the camps. This

1. This account was first published in *Demokratsia*, 15 May 1990. Strictly speaking, Iosifov did not belong to the "other side," but instead to what Primo Levi has called the "gray zone" of the camps, and was himself clearly a victim. He was an inmate like the others, and had a quota to fill. But at the same time his position as

time around I wouldn't survive even two hours. But what's most important, now, is to make the truth known. The whole truth and nothing but the truth. Anyone with even a bit of good sense only has to think about the stakes: who to love, who to hate, who to vote for. . . .

First, let me say a few words about the more distant past— otherwise, you'll never make sense of what followed. We weren't blind to what had led up to 9 September 1944, and what it was leading to. I'd been at the first Communist meeting the day before in Varna, when the first Soviet planes and tanks arrived. We could hear gunfire from the room where we were meeting. It was then that Dana Murdanlarska, whose husband had been found guilty of sabotage and hanged in prison, shot the commander of the Third Army, General Christov, point blank while he was in the act of turning power over to the newly installed Fatherland Front. This was our first impression of our "liberators," and immediately after we saw what justice meant to the Communists.

In 1947, I was sent to a Work Reeducation Center near Nozharevo. There were three or four other camps in the vicinity. Most of us in the camp were political prisoners. But I wasn't even a member of a political party, nor was my father. No, we weren't against those in power. But that hardly mattered: it was enough to be disagreeable in order to be declared an enemy and sent off to camp.

I see in *Duma*, which I read regularly, that the Party is ridding itself of the sadists and the rest of the filth that ran the camps.[2] But who was behind all of this? Who sent people like me to these camps?

---

nurse gave him certain privileges and sometimes drew him toward the other end of the "zone." There are numerous testimonies to his general lack of medical knowledge; according to one former prisoner, "There was a nurse in the camp, but when we went to see him, he'd treat us with a club. He'd pull teeth with pliers and a white hot screwdriver" (Alexander Zlatarev, *Den*, 9 April 1990). Another prisoner recounts that he was beaten by the brigade chief Dimitŭr Tsvetkov and Zhoro: "I was pounded into a bloody pulp by the two of them. They thought I was dead, and they had me tossed with the other corpses behind the latrine. But another prisoner saw me and gave me some water, which revived me" (*The Survivors*). This did not prevent Zhoro from becoming himself a target of Gazdov's hatred, however. Following his liberation, he pursued his taste for the practical side of medicine and is now a healer and diviner.

2. *Duma* is the official paper of the former Bulgarian Communist Party.

Did we send ourselves? It was the members of the neighborhood
Communist organizations who had us arrested: the folks at the
Fatherland Front, the local police—in short, it was the Party that
sent us to the camps. Any woman of easy virtue could get rid of
her husband by sending him off to camp—and there were women
who did so. In fact, anyone who wanted for whatever reason to
make someone else's life a living hell could do so. The system made
it possible.

I escaped from Nozharevo after a few months. It wasn't difficult; one could escape from just about anywhere. For example, I
eventually ended up at Belene, on the Persin Island. A group of us
was sent to Sofia in order to work on the Pioneers' Palace. The
director was Kina Spasova, who was the wife of Mircho Spasov.
One day I was worked over by the guards and was told that I was
going to be sent back to Belene and that I'd never leave again alive.
I escaped that same night. A few months later, I was arrested again
and sent back to Belene. Four months of disciplinary treatment: I
think it's a record that no one has ever beaten. My life was saved by
another inmate, Andrei Georgiev from the city of Stanke Dimitrov.
He was the camp nurse. The daily work quota was beyond the power
of most of the camp slaves, and if Andrei had not slipped me a bowl
of beans and bread, I'd never have survived. Out of gratitude, I'd
give him a hand in the infirmary. I became a sort of stretcher-bearer,
which came in handy later on.

When the camp at Belene was closed, we "hoodlums" were
taken to Lovech. There were 160 men and 14 women. We found just
three inmates at the camp. I was a hoodlum, the father of the singer
Bogdana Karadocheva was a hoodlum, the well-known lawyer Zlatko was a hoodlum, the musician Sasha "Dearheart" was a hoodlum,
the politician Lyuben Boyanov was a hoodlum . . . we were all hoodlums. And they killed us off like flies.

Like everyone else, I dug up rock in the quarry. But I also ban-
daged fifty, one hundred, two hundred people a day. The prisoners
were covered with wounds, as deep as two centimeters and filled
with white worms. I'd pull out the worms with small sticks, since I
didn't have any other instrument. I watched the father of the cyclist

Nencho Christov die: he refused to be hospitalized and died of uremia. In January 1960 or 1961, they killed Ivan Bŭrzakov. It seems that he was against collectivization. The poor fellow.... I've heard stories of heroism and horror, I've read Dante's *Inferno*, but they pale in comparison to what I saw at Lovech the day they killed Bŭrzakov. In the courtyard they tied him to a pole near the infirmary. It was unbearably cold, but Bŭrzakov was dressed only in a pair of army fatigues, a shirt, and was barefoot. The brigade chiefs filed past him, each of them pouring a bucket of water over his head. Can you imagine that? To tie a man to a pole and freeze him alive? Yet, four days later he was still alive.

Finally, one of the officers shouted, "Why are you keeping him tied to the pole like that? Take him to the quarry to work!" When Bŭrzakov was untied, he fell to the ground. They tied a rope to his feet, and we were ordered to drag him behind us. He was dragged on the ground to the quarry and back. This lasted two days. His head bounced against the stones. He died the second day....

Even the most powerful members of the Party now say that the camps were filled with the dregs of society. They're absolutely right: the Party did send scum to Lovech—but they were the ones dressed in uniforms. The only one I can speak well of is Lieutenant Trifonov, who was a doctor. As for Gazdov, Chakŭrov ("the Clubfooted Devil"), Mircho Spasov, and the others, they all stood there, watching over us with watches in hand, timing us as we loaded the wagons full of stone. Sasha "Dearheart" was brought there at 11:30, taken to Gazdov's office and then to the quarry. At 4:30 that afternoon, his body was carted back, with his socks stuffed into his mouth. Vasil Marinski, a doctor who belonged to the Party, was also brought to the camp. He was sent to the quarry, and when he was brought back, his blood pressure was 28/14.5. I barely saved his life. Afterward, he approached Gazdov and lied about me so that he could take my position, which was preferable to the quarry.[3] I barely survived the beating that followed.

3. Doctor Marinski appears in a number of other prisoner accounts and does not seem to have been playing both sides of the camp. But it is true that he replaced Zhoro, who was eminently unqualified for the post of camp nurse.

Anani was named brigade chief, but he wouldn't hit the prisoners under him. This seems to be why he was himself clubbed to death. Another inmate threw himself under the train, and both his legs were cut off. He was written off for dead and thrown into a sack. I opened the sack to help him, but they beat him to death and worked me over as well.[4] Those who were involved were all ex-criminals: Shakho the Gypsy, Levordashki, Blago the Donkey, Dimitŭr Tsvetkov, Dzhokata, Tsanko Terziev. . . .

One day a father and son were brought to the camp, Ivan and Gencho Gospodinov from Sofia. Gazdov told them, "You'll never get out of here alive." One day the son was killed, and the father followed him the next day. Lyuben Boyanov, an Agrarian deputy from Pazardzhik, was also brought to the camp. Pointing at Boyanov, Gazdov told Shakho: "I don't want to see this man again." That same night Shakho reported back to Gazdov: "It's done—the bastard has been taught his lesson." The following morning at roll call, Gazdov saw Lyuben Boyanov standing in one of the rows. He began to scream at Shakho for having lied to him. It turned out that Shakho had mistakenly killed Lyuben Paunov from Samokov. He corrected the error the next day: we found Lyuben Boyanov stuffed into a sack. Every day the rest of us expected to end up in a sack, too.

The newspapers have been publishing stories about the camps, but up until now, all we've seen is the tip of the iceberg. It would be a good thing if the Party were not allowed to get away with this by fobbing off the responsibility onto a handful of low-ranking bastards. The real assassins are Gazdov, Gogov, Goranov,

---

4. Another inmate has recounted this same event: "One day while we were loading a train, the wagon had to be shifted, and Pesho took advantage of the movement by throwing himself under the wheels. His two legs were cut off, above the knees. Three of us ran over and pulled him out. We called for Zhoro, the nurse. He replied, 'He can't be saved.' I then heard Pesho say, 'I want to be legless, so that I can go back home.' He began to black out, and Zhoro ran to the tool shop at the quarry and brought back a metal pin. He then plunged it into Pesho's heart, so that he wouldn't continue to suffer. That same night Zhoro was beaten by the guards, who were angry that he had ended Pesho's suffering. There were four of them, and they took turns beating the living daylights out of Zhoro. It was the first time I saw him beaten. He was usually left alone, since he was a strong fellow who worked a lot" (*The Survivors*).

Neshev, Chakŭrov, Mircho Spasov. Why are the people in power hiding? All we are shown are the monster's tentacles, while the head remains hidden. How many rocks did I dig up at Lovech for these people? They should have been used to build a monument. At Buzludzha, for example. Or perhaps the Berlin Wall....

Yes, I'd willingly dig up rocks again if they were used to build a monument to commemorate the dead of all the camps. Or used as a gravestone for the Party that created them. The Bulgarian Communist Party! I know that there are decent people in the Party, but we all need to know the truth. We need to know about the hell that was Lovech so that fascism and Communism will never again exist. Pushing a man to kill his own brother with a club: this took place at Lovech, too. The individuals responsible for this—were they really men? Gogov, Gazdov—they were Communists....

It's been reported that those who were killed in the dead of winter at Lovech had "heat stroke" given as the cause on the death certificates, while those who died in the summer were victims of "flu."[5] Well, I'm the one who wrote these certificates. Knowingly. Deliberately. It was neither ignorance nor the wish to hide the truth. You see, we couldn't write the truth at the time. If I had, I'd have been put in a sack myself. I always hoped that one day others would read these certificates and ask themselves how such absurd diagnoses came about. And that this would eventually lead them to the truth about these deaths, about Lovech, about the Bulgarian Communist Party ... the time has come.

5. In fact, there are seven death certificates that give the cause of death as "heat stroke," and seven others "flu." There are many others that attribute the cause of death to "heart attack" or "lung-related problems."

S E V E N

A Brigade Chief

BLAGOY GAYTANSKI

—*Mr. Gaytanski, you were arrested simply because you were friendly with the children of wealthy parents who were against the Communists. How is it that you became a brigade chief at Lovech?*[1]

—I didn't have a choice. And besides, I quickly saw that a brigade chief could actually soften the lot of the men for whom he was responsible. At the "silos," where I oversaw my workers, there

---

1. This interview was published in *Demokratsia*, 14 May 1990. Blagoy Gaytanski, known as Blago the Donkey, was assigned to a series of camps (Kofaldzha, Belene, Lovech) from 1947 to 1962. It was at Lovech that he served as a brigade chief, responsible for overseeing the work of his fellow prisoners (and thus the equivalent of the kapo in the Nazi camps). According to the accounts of other prisoners, he was one of the harshest brigade chiefs.

were no murders, but just a few regrettable accidents that I wish had never happened.

—*Still, there were occasions when you punished men in your unit.*

—Yes, unfortunately. But I suffered as much as the fellow who was punished. This is what would happen: the guilty party was forced to lie down on the ground, and we'd hit him with our sticks. This was done only when ordered by the guards, who would watch to make sure that the punishment was carried out. The inmates had to be intimidated in order to work and fill their quotas.

—*Where did this punishment take place?*

—Behind a rock at the quarry, so that the civilian workers would not learn about the camp rules.

—*Do you know that former prisoners call you an assassin?*

—Yes, I know. Obviously, many people were envious of my situation and are now taking advantage of the inquests in order to slander my name and take their revenge. But don't forget those whose wounds I cleaned and who also have stories to tell about me. These prisoners were like children to me: I wanted them to work, to fill their quota, so they wouldn't be beaten in front of the camp gates.

—*Mr. Gaytanski, this is an interview, not an inquest. And so, could you tell us if you're at peace with your conscience?*

—Oh, yes, completely. And I think that the truth will come out that the guilty ones were not us.

EIGHT

Two Guards

SOKOL RALCHEV

It was in 1962 when a local Party official asked me if I'd ever considered joining the police.[1] I thought, "Well, why not?" and went to Lovech in order to apply for a position at the personnel office. I was asked where I'd done my military service, and I replied that during my first year I served in the engineering corps as a telegraph operator. "Ah, that's fine," I was told. "You're just the sort of recruit we're looking for. Fill out your application and you'll hear from us." About a month later, I was called back to Lovech. I'd requested a position in the city of Lovech and didn't even know at the time that the camp actually existed. That's to say, I'd heard about such a

1. This section is taken from the documentary film *The Survivors*.

camp, but had no idea what was going on inside of it. When I showed up, I was told that I'd been accepted and was given a contract to sign. I did as I was told, and signed a contract for three years. I was then told, "Listen, my boy, for the moment we haven't any openings in town. And so you'll begin your assignment at the Sun Coast—the rock quarry—while waiting for a position to open up here."

With that, I was given a machine gun—even though I was still in civilian clothing—along with a hundred cartridges. "We'll drive you to the quarry in the police wagon." It must have been about noon when we arrived. I reported to the section officer and commander of the guards, Captain Baev. "And so, you're the new recruit ..." "Yes, I am." He filled me in on camp regulations. Letters must not be allowed into the camp, nor must they be allowed to be sent.... Detail after detail. That same night, I was assigned to a watch at the second guard tower, located behind the prisoners' barracks. The inmates were all still at the quarry. As I was walking to the tower with Adjutant Romanov, he pointed out three corpses.... He told me, "Don't be scared by the bodies in the sacks: they're all dead. Just so that you know." I replied, "Sure." But I couldn't stop looking at the corpses in the sacks once I began standing guard. There was a moment when I was sure that one of them moved. Maybe I'd been staring too long and hard at the sacks. Anyway, I pressed the alarm button, and Romanov came running up. "What is it, my boy?" "Well, I think one of the bodies moved." "What are you talking about? Do the dead move?" He then had Baev transfer me to the guard post no. 1 to finish out my stint. From there, that same night, I first saw how the prisoners were brought back to camp under armed guard....

There was a roll call. I watched how it worked. The prisoners were lined up and ordered to stand at attention. Everybody did so, and one man—I think his name was Pantalei—called out all of the names from a list. He'd begin, "Ivan, Dragan." And the prisoner would have to step forward and under the light in order to make sure it was him. It wasn't like the army, where you answer "Here, here." Following this ceremony, those who didn't meet the day's quota had to step forward. They were then forced to lie on their stomachs, and someone ordered, "Give them the shovels!" And the guards would begin to hit the prisoners on the ground because they hadn't filled their quota. They were then told, "Don't bother filling the quota tomorrow if you want more of the same. Get your ass to the barracks!" A brigade chief was standing by the door to the barracks, and as the prisoners passed, he'd hit them with his stick. It was the same process to get them out of the barracks in the morning....

The prison guards weren't unfeeling toward the inmates. Some of us were sympathetic, while others weren't. Don't forget that I was still young when all of this was going on. At first, I was scared. My duty was to stand guard at the camp.... When I was sent to the quarry, I'd watch what Shakho the Gypsy, the one who hit the hardest, was doing to the inmates. Along with another fellow, he was chasing the prisoners. He was a monster.

I'd seen films on the German camps, and I didn't see much of a difference between them and Lovech. The camp was filled with prisoners paralyzed by fear. The beatings were so systematic and brutal that the prisoners wondered if they would ever leave alive. They'd been imprisoned without ever being condemned, and they never knew if they'd survive or not. But in any event, there they were, inside the camp. There were many deaths. There was one fellow who played the violin and was called Paganini. He'd say, "My Lord, please take me from this living hell: call me to your side." And called he was. He died in Lovech.

I recall one instance when it was still winter—it was damned cold, snowing and windy—and we were all wearing greatcoats. There was one inmate who wasn't working, and we were ordered: "Strip him naked to the belt." In that weather. It was terrible. There he was, naked in the snow ... because he couldn't work any more.

NIKOLAS IVANOV

In order to maintain internal security at Lovech, there were more than a dozen guards whose job was to make sure that orders were obeyed while the prisoners were at work.[2] I belonged to this detachment. I carried a pistol, which I always kept hidden so that it wouldn't be seen, but placed so that it could easily be reached in case of emergency. During the nine months that I served, up till the closing of the camp, I didn't have to pull the gun out even once.

The camp commander's major fear was that, in case of revolt, the inmates would try to take our weapons. This is why, when we were in direct contact with them, we were lightly armed. On the other hand, the policemen at the camp carried pistols, machine guns, and clubs. I'd often ask them why they carried clubs. I'd ask and ask, but never got an answer that made sense. Maybe the club was a humanitarian weapon, a warning that it would be followed by their guns.... But as far as I know, that point was never reached. It would have been a waste of ammunition.

Personally, I never had any problems with the inmates. In my opinion, there was no real danger of rebellion. They were so terrified ... and too weak. Exhausted, crippled, covered with wounds and bruises ... in rags, reeking from filth.... Their impotence was terrible. A single blow could easily kill one of them. But how could a human being kill someone in that state? Especially if the prisoner was a woman? But they killed them anyway! It was the police! I never understood why. Maybe out of fear, which was easily stirred up ... maybe. I never saw them kill the inmates. The police were careful when they were around us, and there was a lot of tension between the two groups.

The inmates worked at a number of sites: the quarry, the Interior Ministry's villa, the Party's villa, the cooperatives in the surrounding towns, as well as at the Party headquarters in Lovech. Why were they deported? I can't say: I didn't read the files. I only knew what I was told, as well as rumors and what my colleagues said. Many of the prisoners were cultivated—these were the political inmates, I guess. Doctors, engineers, judges, managers ... there was even a resistance fighter against fascism. There were those who didn't know why they were there, others who were there because

2. This section was published in *Demokratsia*, 2 April 1990.

their wives were beautiful ... others because of shady dealings that threatened people in high places ... or others who were there simply because their pants fit too tight or because they were caught telling political anecdotes. There were also actual criminals, but they were employed as brigade chiefs and kept order in the barracks and so forth. They were willing to do anything necessary in order to hold on to their privileges. It seems they were the ones who hit the hardest. Shakho, of course, belonged to this group. He was always standing by the door with a club in his hand, keeping an eye out.

In my opinion, the inmates were murdered at night. In the evening, when I'd return home (I was newly married at the time and did my best to disappear as quickly as possible), a table was set up on the porch of the administrative building, facing the esplanade and barracks, and the camp commanders would sit down for yet another bout of drinking. There were Major Gogov, who was the camp commander, Captain Baev, who commanded the police, Lieutenant Gazdov, who was from the Bureau of State Security, and the Red Major, the biggest bastard and murderer of all, who later died like a dog. The inmate who was in charge of the canteen, Dako, told me how they'd go through staggering amounts of food and drink. After getting completely drunk, they'd entertain themselves by torturing inmates or assaulting women prisoners.

On my way to work in the morning, I'd pass enormous pools of blood: it looked like a slaughterhouse. I'd ask what had happened, but I'd never get an answer.

Some of the women prisoners were beautiful, though it was difficult to tell, since they were so filthy and horribly neglected. You felt like retching when you walked past them. Still, the policemen raped them regularly. When we heard that the camp was going to be closed, the inmates' regimen was improved a bit, and the women started to complain about their maltreatment. That's when Gogov ordered me to guard them while they worked. Gogov began to complain about the policemen, most of whom came from Belene. He said that they were out of control, but this isn't true: Gogov had a great deal of power. I think he was simply trying to wash his hands of what had happened. He was a crafty man who knew which strings to pull: he left Gazdov to take care of the dirty work and went to Sofia for instructions. I don't think he was the sole instigator of the murders at Lovech. The people "upstairs" knew what was happening. As for the policemen, they had gotten used to this sort of behavior at Belene.... And they couldn't break the habit. For them, killing had become a duty, a daily task ... a skill. They even believed that they were acting according to an official order. But no one could say from whom or where this order had come.

Since the inmates were working at the building site of the Party headquarters in Lovech, as well as in the neighboring villages, the locals saw them and became increasingly upset. In addition, the trains passed along the edge of the quarry and would occasionally come to a stop. The foreigners on board would then take photos of what they saw. Following the visit of an official commission, it became clear that the camp was going to be closed. The inmates refused to believe it. When the women with whom I was working heard the news, they began to cry and pray. They suspected that it was all a show so that they could be murdered more easily. The women were taken to the village of Skravena, while the men were liberated at Lovech itself.

At a certain point, all the commanding officers disappeared. The only one left was the Red Major, who kept his distance and, with a backpack tossed over his shoulder, was happy to spend his time hiking and camping in the surrounding countryside. During the last days of its existence, the camp was run by us guards. We were then dispersed to the four corners of Bulgaria. And there you have it....

I was in the camp for nine months. They were the least terrible months at Lovech, hardly anything at all compared to what had taken place before.... Still, I had seen enough to stay with me for the rest of my life.

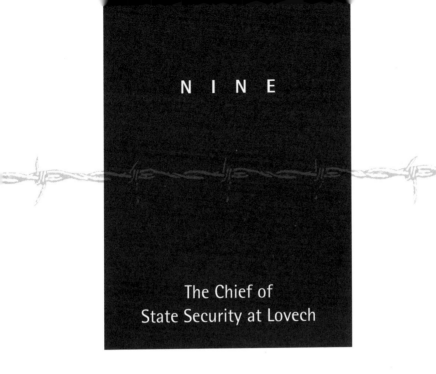

N I N E

The Chief of State Security at Lovech

NIKOLAS GAZDOV

—*Mr. Gazdov, you know why you have been asked to appear. When did you begin your assignment at the camp of Lovech?*[1]
    —14 July 1960.
    —*How many people were then in the camp?*
    —Oh, I can't recall. It was so long ago. . . .
    —*Where had you been before taking up your duties at Lovech?*

---

1. This chapter is taken from the documentary film *The Survivors*. In this segment, filmed in 1990, Gazdov is testifying before an inquiry commission on the concentration camps. A former partisan and "resistance fighter against fascism," Gazdov was head of State Security at Lovech. He was thus directly responsible for the terror that ran wild at the camp. As we have seen, all of the inmate accounts point

—At Belene. I started there on 6 April 1957 in the capacity of secretary to the camp commander. I was a civilian then.

—*Tell us what happened from the moment you arrived till the moment when you were fired and left the camp.*

—I was one of those who'd been singled out.[2] Well, it was like this ... I'll tell you what I can remember. A group of women at Belene were entrusted to me. I had to "take care" of them. Which is what I did as long as they were there. Some of them were political prisoners, and they were kept apart. They were freed in 1958, and only the common criminals remained.[3]

—*How many people passed through the camp during the period you worked there?*

—Well, there were less than eight hundred people. But I'm guessing, of course.

—*Do you remember approximately how many deaths there were during this same period?*

—No, I don't remember. I've been reading about these things in the papers. No. I don't remember this sort of thing. So many years have passed....

—*Do the accounts you have been reading or seeing on the television help you remember what happened?*

—All that I remember is that the same questions were asked during the official inquiry ... and I think I responded fully at the time.

—*But you are not responding fully now.*

---

to Gazdov and underscore his personal taste for torture. One inmate recounts, "I'll never forget how Gazdov humiliated us. One summer, he brought his wife and child to the camp so that they'd see what a hero he was. The entire family welcomed us at the gate of the camp one night as we were returning from the quarry. We were carrying back the body of a boy named the Cock, who had been from Burgas. Gazdov asked Shakho what had happened. When Shakho said he didn't know, Gazdov replied, 'Ah, you know, a little bird is telling me that you killed him.' And then he laughed in front of his child" (Alexander Zlatarev, *Den,* 9 April 1990).

2. Following a number of complaints and inquiries in 1961 and 1962, Gazdov was fired. But he was never tried or troubled in any manner.

3. This does not correspond to the truth, but can be explained by the common practice of the State Security apparatus: "political prisoners" were described as "hoodlums," hence common criminals.

—Which question haven't I answered fully?

—*The last one. Roughly, how many deaths were there? Ten? Twenty?*

—No, no, there were about a hundred deaths. During the period I was there—for the entire period. I know there were deaths, but can't say how many, since I didn't keep a list.

—*Who did keep count of the deaths, then?*

—The adjutants had the lists of those who died in the camp. I myself never wrote anything down.

—*And who signed these reports?*

—The reports? The camp director.

—*And were you the director?*

—No, it was Gogov.

—*Before you arrived, had there been any deaths? Do you know?*

—I heard that there had been, but I couldn't tell, since I wasn't there. People also went on dying after I left. Most of the people who died in the camps where barely alive when they were brought in from the police stations. They could hardly walk. And when the sun is blazing against the rocks, the end is near. I'm a human being, too, and I was there and knew what it was like. The weakest inmates couldn't withstand this hard work in the sun. I know everything about Lovech because all the files passed through my hands. All of them. The police stations sent pretty thick files.

—*In your opinion, was this the only cause of death?*

—There's something else. There were criminals assigned to guard the others and each night . . .

—*Could the brigade chiefs who had been selected by you take someone's life without your knowledge or permission?*

—We weren't told when they beat the prisoners. . . . As for the rock quarry, in particular, I rarely went there. My work was mostly at camp, where there was . . .

—*Didn't you have to provide an explanation for each death? A man dies. Wasn't it your responsibility to explain the circumstances of the death?*

—We were never given such an order. Nobody ever ordered

us to explain what had happened. People knew why back then, and I know why now: the inmates died from being overworked. Some from heatstroke, others from health problems. Ah, there's no two ways about it: the work was hard.

—*Did you ever take part in the beating of inmates?*

—No, never. Never. The others can say what they want. What I read in the papers makes me sick to my stomach. There are those who say, Gogov beat me, Gazdov beat me, Goranov beat me, so-and-so beat me. I never saw an officer beat anyone whomsoever. Nor did I ever hit anyone.

—*Not among the officers but among the inmates themselves, were there people who would beat others?*

—The inmates ... they'd often fight.

—*Did these frequent fights ever result in deaths?*

—No.

—*Not a single death?*

—I never saw one.

—*Would the inmates ever be punished for fighting? Who did you punish when you learned about these fights? Fighting was forbidden!*

—I never punished anyone, because ...

—*How is that?*

—The fights never ended in deaths.

—*Mr. Gazdov, how did you gather the necessary information concerning possible escape attempts or uprisings in the camp? How and through whom?*

—I had reliable sources, who would keep me informed.

—*Who chose these sources?*

—I did.

—*Were they former employees of State Security?*

—They reported to me on what was happening in the camp because I was an officer with State Security. They were informers, and they kept me informed. That's something you couldn't understand, at least now.

—*Among these individuals, was there at least one whose job was to beat the inmates?*

—Nobody was named to this job at the camp.

—*No, not named.*

—How's that?

—*Assigned, not named.*

—There was no one assigned to such a position.

—*Were they given a lightened workload in return?*

—Who?

—*Your informers.*

—What sort of lightened workload?

—*Certain privileges, for example.*

—This sort of thing didn't take place.

—*Then why would they inform?*

—Through conscientiousness.

—*While you were there, about one hundred people died.*

—I've already told you how they died.

—*It is also obvious that you protected other individuals. But since they are no longer protecting you, stop protecting them.*

—Listen, either you don't want to understand me or I'm not making myself clear. There's no reason for me to protect anyone, because everyone must look after themselves. That's how I see the world. As for what concerns me, no one came to me and said, "Listen, we want to see one hundred people die, we want to see two hundred die, we want to see so-and-so die...." Nothing of the sort was ever said. Now ...

—*Excuse me, but what do you think was the purpose of these camps? Why were they built? Who built them? Why?*

—At the time, and even today, I was persuaded that this was the government's business. The Political Bureau. No one could do this single-handedly, because I saw the costs—the money, I mean—for feeding these people and so on. And so this was a decision that I could not make. In the newspapers, once again, I learn that ... I read that an order from the Council of Ministers was behind all of this ... and that G. Tsankov was put in charge.[4]

4. At the time, Tsankov was minister of the interior. His account is on pages 163–64.

—*Who set the rules down for the harsh nature of this system?*
—Who? It was Mircho Spasov.[5] Mircho Spasov set the rules. Petŭr Gogov, the camp director, told me so.
—*It was Mircho Spasov who fixed the work quota, not you?*
—Yes.
—*Did you inform him that the quota was inhuman?*
—I knew it was, but I didn't dare object, because Mircho Spasov's response would have been simple: "Clear out."

5. Spasov was vice-minister of the interior at the time. His account is on pages 159–63.

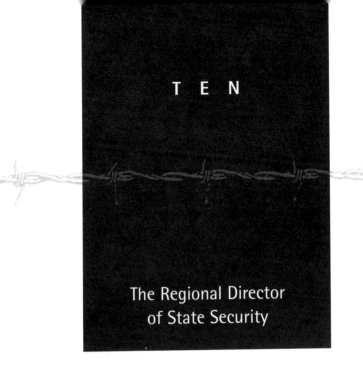

T E N

The Regional Director
of State Security

KIRIL ALEXANDROV

The running of the camp was never, either by its structure or by its organization, under the control of my headquarters in Lovech.[1] I didn't have the right—and I never contested this absence of power—to give orders, to impose a system, or to name individuals to various posts. The camp management provided me with explanations, while I was directly responsible to the Office of Internment and Deportation in Sofia. This was the extent of the structural and organizational ties between my headquarters and the camp management.

1. This chapter is taken from the documentary film *The Survivors*. The film director asked the questions. Alexandrov was director of State Security for the region of Lovech. The camp did not fall within his charge (instead, it was managed directly by Interior); nevertheless, Alexandrov decided on the distribution of the camp workforce at the various work sites in the area.

I never inspected the camp or its management; I never toured the barracks; I never put my feet inside the quarry where they worked. I went there because the bigwigs in Lovech wanted workers, and I asked the camp director to provide the manpower for a couple of building sites. We especially needed workers for ... the villa we were building for the Ministry of the Interior. You see, workers came from different districts: Nikopol, Pleven ...

— *Yes, well, all the same, when you went to the camp, did you get an idea of the atmosphere and the way it was being run?*

— You may find it incredible and think that I'm not telling the truth, but I didn't pay attention to the way the camp was run. I've already told you that I had no responsibilities in this area.

— *But didn't you have any indications or evidence on the running of the camp? Because I myself remember hearing about Lovech when I was young: I didn't have to be the interior minister to know about the horrors that were taking place there, about the simple existence of the camp.*

— During the entire length of my assignment at Lovech, no one said to me, "Alexandrov, this is how the camp is being run ... horrors are being committed, what is going on is terribly wrong, do something if you can." There was a departmental committee at Lovech, to which I belonged. Camp affairs were never raised at the committee meetings. I was an outsider at Lovech. The Party secretary, the mayor, the local chief of police, along with the other bureaucrats, were all local officials: it was easier to tell them to do something. But the question of the camp's operation was never raised either by the first secretary, for example, or by the president of the council (on which I also served).

— *Didn't people begin to recognize the jeep that transported the corpses to Belene? Wasn't it necessary to take certain measures in order to hide what was going on? Weren't people talking?*

— No, no! This never came up.[2]

2. This is not the case. Spasov and Chakŭrov sent the following memo to their subordinates: "The truck [used to transport the bodies], which is recognized by everyone, must be disguised, and disguised often. A truck or jeep can also be borrowed from the regional director [of State Security] at Lovech in order to vary things.

—During this entire time you really had no idea that people were being killed over there?

—Only once did someone tell me that there were a lot of deaths, but not that they were being killed. It was Mircho Spasov. He called me and said, "You know, Alexandrov, there've been a lot of deaths over there. Would you check into it?" I was taken somewhat aback by the request, since he had his own people, who reported directly to him. But this was perhaps a few days before the arrival of the commission that was going to make inquiries about the situation of the inmates. . . .

—There had been no discussions concerning the fact that it was already known that dead inmates were being transported? That rumors were flying? Wasn't a decision made to take certain steps?

—Well, yes, it's possible that there were discussions, but they never reached me. I've told you what my ties were to the camp. Besides, you need to remember the context at the time. For example, when students occupy the universities today, the police leave them alone. Do you think it was the same back then? What I mean is that, back then, we had a different view of the camp and inmates. It was a global view.

—Okay. As a man of this period, what was your view, then, of the existence of these camps?

—You know better than I do what was behind the creation of the camps. The camp at Lovech wasn't the only one, right? As far as I can tell, every foreign crisis—the Suez war, the Middle East . . .

—The events in Hungary . . .

—Yes, the events in Hungary. As for the camp at Lovech, the newspapers have discussed the reasons why the camp was necessary.

—But how do you—someone who lived during this period— explain all of this?

Contact Comrade Alexandrov, regional director of the Interior Ministry, and Comrade Gogov in order to discuss the details of what needs to be done so that this operation can be kept relatively secret, at least during the actual transportation and burial, though nothing illegal is being done. Take action. (Signed), Mircho Spasov" (*The Survivors*).

—Well, again, let me tell you ... as someone who lived through these events.... It was a decision made by more powerful authorities. We saw things differently back then, not like now, with, say, popular dissent and so forth. Especially the bureaucrats who worked in the Ministry of the Interior. We were taught to obey. The decision was made to open the camps. The camp at Lovech was created for hardened criminals, even if there were also innocent people there. Maybe ten years later, while on leave, I learned that one of my colleagues—a comrade who had fought in the resistance—had a son who was a troublemaker. In order to teach him a lesson, he had him sent to Lovech. He died there.

—*Despite all of this, didn't you find it odd—as a Communist—that these individuals, as hardened as they might have been, were never sentenced and didn't have police records?*

—Sure, this is what everyone is now going on about. How was I supposed to find all of this odd when, as I've already told you, I was only taking orders? They made the decisions; they opened this or that camp. I knew, for example, that the running of a camp was very strict. I knew that. I've already told you I didn't know the precise nature of the camp's operation and I wasn't in a position to propose things. The camp's directors didn't answer to me. I had other things to take care of. The only time I dealt with the camp was when the president of the departmental council or the mayor needed workers. We were building the local headquarters for the Party, the offices for the departmental council, the villa....

—*Yes, all right, but let me ask another question. What if you had been a member of the Political Bureau at the time—in other words, placed at the highest level of power? As a Communist, and given the way things were seen back then, would you have gone along with the camps? Would you have thought it opportune? I'm simply trying to understand.*

—In order to answer this, let's take the example of Traycho Kostov.[3].... Traycho Kostov was much more important than those who were in the camps—even if they were men who had their rights

---

3. Communist leader who was executed in 1949 for "treason."

and so forth. Kostov was murdered. At the same time, people were arrested with whom I'd been in prison, with whom I'd been in camp, where they were tortured. We thought they were our enemies.

—*Did you really believe this? Or were you afraid?*

—Afraid? What should we have been afraid of?

—*Well, from the moment the comrades in whom you believed were tortured...*

—Yes, but ... they're issuing reports and so forth. Enemies and agents in the hire of foreign countries—America, Great Britain —who were we to believe? How were we to know? We're speaking about the past, aren't we? You need to understand that this is how we spoke of our authority at the Interior Ministry. We were the sword of the revolution. There was no place for analysis: we simply obeyed orders. I'll tell you once again: the question whether the camps were necessary or not was never asked.

—*And so what should we do today?*

—First of all, we must establish the political responsibility for those who decided to build the camps and imposed the rules for their operation and so forth. As for those who carried out the orders, personal responsibility must be established for those who overstepped their rights, who revealed sadistic tendencies and acted criminally.

—*What do you mean by political responsibility? Must they face trial? Or should we limit ourselves to political reprimands?*

—It's not for me to say. If Ceausescu was condemned for genocide, then we have to judge them. If one considers his case to have been a genocide against his own people, then we can also take our leaders to court.

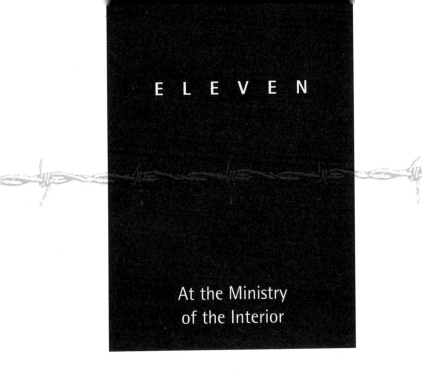

ELEVEN

At the Ministry
of the Interior

MIRCHO SPASOV

—*Who created the camp near Lovech? How, when, and why was it done?*[1]

—It wasn't Mircho Spasov who was behind it. As best as I can remember, Georgi Tsankov, who was then interior minister, gave us the task of creating the camp during a meeting of the Council [of

1. This section was published in *Anteni,* 4 April 1990. Mircho Spasov was the vice-minister of the interior in charge of the camps. As we have seen, he directly inspired the operation of the camps. Born in 1911, he joined the Communist Party in 1932. He was in the resistance during the war, during which he was arrested and interned in a concentration camp. He was quickly promoted in the Party after the war, and in 1948 he was sent to the USSR for a "specialized" education. Upon his return, he put his training to use when he assumed the operation of political repression in Bulgaria.

Ministers], to which I belonged as vice-minister. This was how things usually took place. This duty was assigned to a central ministerial division that oversaw camp internment and deportation. It was Division ID 0789. Work began in February 1959, when it was decided that the camp at Belene would only imprison condemned criminals. All the other inmates would be transferred to Lovech—to the quarry, which I didn't choose and whose location I didn't know.

The camp's organization was given to the relevant sections: the offices of the Interior Ministry at Lovech and Pleven. The camp's regulations were designed to be severe, even cruel, I'd say. It was designed for convicts. Mircho Spasov wasn't responsible for this regime either, or for the boys who were assigned as guards and the camp directors. These instructions all came from above—in other words, the Political Bureau of the Party and the Council of Ministers.

The category of camp to which Lovech belonged has already been indicated: the people who were sent there were never tried or sentenced. There were also people who had been tried—I remember one who had been tried sixty-four times, but he had been sent to the camp without having been sentenced. Given my position at Interior, I would decide if certain individuals would be sent to Lovech or not.

— *Who were those in charge?*

—It was the head of the division, Delcho Chakŭrov. He oversaw the camps and deportations and reported to me. He told me, "We've been notified about a memo that the minister addressed to you." He wrote, "Spasov, how many times must I order you to send so-and-so to Lovech? How am I to interpret this?" There were other notifications of this sort. There were also—how can I say?—notes and messages from the attorney general....

— *Who was the attorney general?*

—At the time, it was Mincho Minchev. According to official practice, the departmental secretary of the Party along with police headquarters and the departmental attorney general sent so-and-so to Lovech along with a dossier. From there, a report would be made to the Division ID 0789, which, in turn, would notify me, reporting that so many new inmates had arrived for such and such reasons.

Everything that took place at Lovech was not only known to Mircho Spasov, who was directly responsible, but also to the first vice-minister, the minister, the upper echelon of the Interior Ministry, and all the police headquarters. The police helped us choose the people who were sent to these camps. Yet, now, in the papers and on the television, the only name that is mentioned is Mircho Spasov!

—*Could you define your own guilt?*

—I admit I'm guilty, but I'm not the only one! I'm guilty for not having taken measures quickly and effectively enough to prevent the sending of people to the camp. I wasn't informed clearly enough and in enough time.[2]

—*Did you have a clear idea of the severity of the camp's organization?*

—I've already answered this question. But, again, I swear that I visited the camp at Lovech just one time, and only for a few minutes.[3] . . . I went to the barracks . . . I didn't think it necessary to go to the quarry while the inmates were working.

—*Is there a difference, according to you, between a severe regime, hard labor, and crime? Crimes, moreover, that have gone unpunished?*

—I was asked the same questions yesterday (27 March 1990) by the Party's Ethics Commission. How can I express myself? I doubt that you'll find someone who'll tell you, in all sincerity, that

2. In 1962, following an inquiry undertaken by the Velchev Commission, Spasov was officially rebuked. But this punishment did not affect his career in the slightest. He kept his post of vice-minister, and that same year he was promoted to the Central Committee and "elected" deputy. He would also be given the highest of decorations (he was awarded the Order of Georgi Dimitrov four times) and named Hero of Socialist Labor. Spasov came under a certain disgrace in 1982, but for unrelated reasons. As director of the Foreign Agreements, he managed an important budget. An inquiry revealed that there was a significant misappropriation of funds. Spasov was called before the Ethics Committee of the Communist Party, which removed him from the Central Committee but without bringing criminal charges against him. Todor Zhivkov intervened personally to ask that Spasov's case be treated leniently.

3. According to the inmates' accounts, Spasov visited the camp, including the quarry, twice a month.

an order was given to beat the prisoners. It's all the less likely that you'll see a vice-minister of the interior like myself go to Lovech and order his subordinates to hit the prisoners.

— *How were the powers of the camp personnel defined?*

— Officially, they were to make sure that the inmates were subjected to hard labor and that there were no escapes. This is at least what I recall.

— *I imagine, without having any proof, that the personnel overstepped their powers....*

— This is what I think as well.

— *Could you now meet face to face the former inmates?*

— No, I couldn't bear it. As far as I'm concerned, they were criminals. There wasn't a single innocent one among them.

— *But didn't you yourself say that they were never sentenced?*

— Veteran criminals were sent there to be isolated. Especially criminals. And hoodlums. It may be true that departmental authorities were too zealous at times and imprisoned people who didn't belong there. The others were among the worst and most incorrigible. They were recidivists.[4] That's the reason that they were there without having been sentenced, that they were picked up because of their actions and sent to Lovech without trial. I can assure you that they were sent to the camp with damning dossiers....

— *How were duties divided among your subordinates?*

— I was responsible for Division ID 0789, which was under my command. At least once a week, I was given a report concerning those arriving at the camp, those who were liberated, official requests to send others to the camp, requests from inmates' families, camp deaths, the use of the inmates as well as the organization ...

— *Who was under the orders of Division ID 0789?*

— Of all the high-ranking camp officers, I only remember Trichkov. He was the highest-ranking officer at Belene and Lovech. Under his orders was the commander of the guards Gogov, Goranov, and Gazdov. They were the last links in the chain of high command.

4. According to a former inmate, during one of his visits to the camp, Spasov declared, "You are the parasites in our garden, and you must be exterminated" (*Pogled*, 2 April 1990).

— What do you think of the responsibility of those in the direct line of command? Should they answer for those acts which exceeded their professional duties?

— Yes, I think so. They've already had to answer for their acts and have been punished, including two who had retired.

GEORGI TSANKOV

— Is it possible that actions were taken in your ministry without your knowledge, even if they fell in your sphere of responsibility?[5]

—I admit that a few isolated cases may have occurred. In such a large ministry, the minister isn't in a position to know everything. This is why he has assistants who run various sectors; my confidence in them was complete. But I need to emphasize that the ministry officials, and I myself as minister, had too many duties of the most varied sort. During this period, many things were considered to be treasonous.

— What role did you play in the creation of the camps at Lovech, Skravena, and elsewhere? What was your attitude toward them? How did you learn that these camps were being built?

—Following the Party plenum in 1956,[6] the decision was made to free all the inmates at Belene. Alongside the political prisoners, there were also many common criminals, who were responsible for the national rise in criminality. Theft, murders, break-ins, rapes had all increased. The population was terrified. The ministry had received many letters of complaint. Women who worked in the afternoon didn't dare go to the factories, because they were harassed on the streets, robbed and attacked. There was also a spate of murders.

Todor Zhivkov also received similar letters. This is why, at a meeting of the Political Bureau, he spoke about the situation in

5. Published in *Duma* (the organ of the former Communist Party) in 1990. Tsankov was minister of the interior from 1951 to February 1962.
6. Officially, this plenum marked the de-Stalinization of the Party. In practice, however, it represented Zhivkov's victory over Chervenkov for control of the Party.

Bulgaria and proposed the creation of this camp where these criminals would be placed.[7] The proposal was unanimously adopted. It
was even welcomed with relief. As minister of the interior, I was
charged with putting the proposal into effect. This is why I called a
meeting of the Council of Ministers, and gave Mircho Spasov the
task of creating and running the camps, since he was already the
director of the section Internment and Deportation.

    —You were removed from the Central Committee and your
vice-ministerial post at the same moment that the camp at Lovech
was closed. Is there a relation between these two events?

    —My removal from the ministry and the Council of Minis-
ters had nothing to do with the camps and prisons. Zhivkov's aim
was to get rid of Yugov[8] and me in order to smooth the creation of
his personality cult. This goal was reached by the coup d'état he led
on the eve of the Eighth Party Congress.

    There is a related issue. Once the crimes committed in the
camps had been revealed and the Velchev Commission was allowed
to investigate freely and without constraints (all the more so when a
few months later I was no longer a member of the Political Bureau
or Central Committee and had been retired at the age of forty-nine),
who would benefit the most by hiding these perversions and crimes?
Who was afraid of their discovery? Why weren't those found guilty
severely punished? Who protected them? This isn't the only case in
which Zhivkov didn't "know" anything. He enjoyed playing the
role of a man who was blind to what was taking place around him!

    —Were you aware of everything that was taking place? Did
you visit the camp? Who determined the way it was run? Did you
report on these camps to the Political Bureau?

    —I learned about the perversions of the law from the Velchev
Commission, and now, thirty years later, from the mass media. I was
never there [i.e., the camp at Lovech]. I had placed my confidence in
those who were in charge. There were jurists among them.

---

    7. The surviving documents indicate that the proposal to open the camps was
made by Tsankov.
    8. Former minister of the interior responsible for the initial stage in the cre-
ation of the camps. At the moment of his removal from power, he was prime minister.

AMONG THE FAMILIES

MARGARITA STOYANOVA

The one time I was able to see my father was with the help of my maternal uncle, who had spent about fifteen years at Enikyoy before 9 September.[1] He took me to Bobov Dol, where my father was in a camp. We went in a carriage; were I to go back now, I'd be completely lost. I remember climbing to what seemed to be an old stockade with barbed wire joined by low stakes. My uncle then asked me if I saw my father. I said, "No, where is he?" I saw a sea of living skeletons covered with skin. They were so miserably dressed, so exhausted, and seemed so terrified. I continued walking, and then my uncle asked again if I didn't recognize my father. I said no.

"There," my uncle said, "he's just next to you." I threw myself around this man's neck, kissed him, and asked if he was really my father and why he'd changed so much. He was dressed in a white shirt, but it wasn't his own. And it wasn't really white: it was a white rag splattered with blood. He was wearing pants that weren't his own either. They were in tatters and barely reached his knees. When I turned around, I saw about ten or fifteen meters away a huge pit that served as the latrine. A man's head was on top of this reeking hole. You see, in the middle of the pit there were two poles and a head, on which there remained only a closed mouth, as white as a mask, and big white worms that were crawling everywhere: in the ears, on the head, everywhere, in the nose. I asked what it was.

"Don't look, my child," my father said.

I never saw him again.

VERA STAMBOLOVA

We were speechless when we left the camp.[2] Since the fate of our loved ones and those near to us depended upon our silence, we

---

1. This section is taken from the documentary film *The Survivors*. During the Second World War, Enikyoy was the principal concentration camp and held in particular a number of Communist resistance fighters.
2. This section is taken from the documentary film *The Survivors*.

didn't dare say a single word. Even those who were closest to us—even our children—didn't dare say that their parents had been in the camps, though we were innocent and were kept there for years without ever being tried or sentenced. We were physical wrecks when we left the camps, covered with sores, and even our loved ones, those closest to our hearts, didn't dare utter a single word on the horrors we experienced in the camp.

My husband never told our son about his experience. Now our son asks me, "Mom, why didn't you ever give me these letters to read? Why didn't you ever show them to me?"

"Ah," I reply, "how could I show them to you when you were leaving for your military service? The men who imprisoned your father were going to give you a weapon, so how was I to show you these letters, which denounced their very crimes?"

My son enrolled in the school Komsomol. Once again, I was prevented from showing him the letters. What can I say? We kept our silence as if we were criminals, and when things improved just a little bit, we counted ourselves blessed.

JACQUELINE DONCHEVA

My father was Nikolai Donchev, the literary critic, a member of the Union of Writers and the Union of Journalists, and editor in chief of the book columns for the Italian and French journals then published in Bulgaria. Shortly after 9 September 1944 he was fired, the publication of the papers halted, and he himself was expelled from both unions. One early morning in November, about two months after the taking of power by the "people's party," four men burst into our apartment. They were wearing black leather jackets, helmets, and had hatred written on their unshaved faces. They were carrying metal bars and used them to break all the bookcases in my father's library. They threw all the books into a pile in the middle of the room and kept repeating, "Fascist books! Only dirty fascists read fascist books!"

Obviously, the "comrades" were nearly illiterate and didn't know the Latin alphabet, since most of the books were written in

French and Italian.[3] After knocking all the books to the ground, they searched the entire apartment. While all of this was happening, the entire family was huddled into a corner and guarded by one of the men. In spasms of hatred or excitement, they would often hit my father, shouting, "Fascist, dirty fascist!" In the years that followed 9 September, "fascist" was the worst insult one could use.

My father was taken away from us on that cold winter morning: hatless, in his suit, and beaten on the back by the metal bars. We weren't allowed to hug or kiss him. I'll never forget my father's look when we were separated: on his face you could read all the pain, the human pride trampled into the ground, so much love and dignity. The days that followed were terrible, for we had no news concerning him. We later learned that about three hundred intellectuals had been arrested on that same day: writers, journalists, painters, professors. Among them were Professor Arnaudov, Ivan Duichev, the writer Dimitûr Talev, and many others.[4]

For three months we learned nothing about those who were arrested. We later learned that they were initially packed like sardines in a garage that had neither light nor heat. They would take turns by group sitting down on the cement floor: one group would remain standing while the other sat or leaned against the floor. They were subsequently transferred to the central prison in Sofia. One cold February morning, my father came home with a bundle of clothing under his arm (we had been allowed to send him some clothing). At first, I didn't recognize him: standing in front of me was an exhausted old man, skinny and badly shaved but in whose eyes there remained an old sparkle. With tears of joy running down my cheeks, I threw myself into his arms. Some of his poems — "In a Cell," "Meditation," "Sonnet," and others—date from this period he was in prison, but they were never published, because of their religious content. Much later, after forty-five years had passed and my father was on his deathbed, he brought back to life a few images from this distant and terrible past.

3. Translator's note: Bulgarian uses the Cyrillic, not Latin, alphabet.
4. These were among the best-known intellectuals in pre- and postwar Bulgaria. Arnaudov was a literature professor, Duichev a medievalist, and Talev a novelist.

I passed high school with flying colors. I wanted to continue my studies at university, but I needed an affidavit from the Fatherland Front in order to enroll for the entrance examination. In order to receive the Party's benediction, I worked the entire year as a volunteer with the Front. I led neighborhood reading clubs, attended meetings, and worked in the brigades. This is how I obtained the papers necessary to apply to university.

I got married during my first year at university. My husband, Ilia Trenev, who was a few years older than I, was a lawyer. At the end of 1950, we had a marvelous little girl! Despite the difficulties in the years after the war—with the shortages, ration tickets, land confiscations, disappearance of people, harassment and persecution, the Popular Tribunals and condemnation—yes, despite all of that, I was very happy. My dreams were coming true: I was a student, a wife, and mother!

But this was the period when the famous "Stalinist" trials began. My husband was one of its victims. Very early in the morning of 4 December, our house was visited by three "comrades" who were dressed in civilian clothing and arrived in a jeep. (The police were already motorized back then.) After searching the house, they took my husband away for a "quick" identification check, which lasted eight years. For a long time, I had no news. We later learned that eight young educated men had been accused of spying on "behalf of the United States." The eight men did not know one another, but all of them had been close friends of the principal suspect, I.D., who was the son of a former police chief. Some of them had met I.D. at the French lycée; the others had met him at law school.

The suspects were subjected to an investigation that lasted for nearly two years. They were denied visitation rights, and couldn't receive food while the "guardians of order" were piecing together their case. Once the accusations were made public, the suspects were placed under a specially designed "fattening-up" regime. We were asked to provide "fortifying" food, money, and, before the trial, civilian clothing (suits, shirts, ties). We had to look respectable, in order to show how the "People's Government" took care of its citizens, even when they were enemies of the people! The day of the trial finally arrived. After two years of separation, my husband and I saw one another once again in the courthouse, though we didn't have the right to speak to or touch one another. We had to limit ourselves to exchanging glances that tried to convey so many different emotions. The trial started with the statements of the suspects. They each offered a self-criticism. They had all learned their lessons perfectly. They were speaking as if they were reading from a script. You can imagine my astonishment when I learned that my husband's spying consisted in giving three pieces of information to the prime suspect: first, that near the tramway stop Ocha Kupel was a textile factory; second, that factory no. 12 was located near the tramway stop Dimitûr Nestorov, which was near our house; and third, that there was a paper factory on the road to Gorna Banya. In light of these accusations, my husband was condemned to ten years of prison and deprived of his civic rights for fifteen years.

The day Ilia was condemned has been branded on my memory. The vast Room 15 was full to bursting. Since it was meant to be didactic, the trial was open to the public. At eleven o'clock, a police detachment brought the guilty individuals through a small side door. They were led to the first row of seats and with eager, worried expressions looked for their families. The room suddenly came to life. A voice cried out, "Stand for the judges." All of the assistants leapt to their feet. Slowly and solemnly, the "venerable magistrates" took their places. The presiding judge was the "popular and respected" S.V., who certainly qualifies for the *Guiness Book of World Records* for the number of death penalties he handed out. It was said that he swam in a sea of human blood. A deathly silence hovered over the room. The heavy atmosphere was broken by the calm, clear, and distinct voice of the presiding judge.

"In the name of the people, in virtue of article . . . the court condemns I.D. to death!"

A barely repressed, heartrending moan came from among the spectators, followed by the sound of a body falling to the ground. The judge's voice continued, "In the name of the people . . . death!" Another groan, another body slumping to the floor. Again, "In the name of the people . . . death!" Same moan, same sound of someone fainting. A fourth time, "In the name of the people ... death!" Someone else moans and collapses to the ground. This was followed by two twenty-year prison sentences, one for fifteen years, and, for my husband, ten years. We could appeal to the Supreme Court. At the end of the trial, the wives of the condemned men were invited to the chambers of the presiding judge. In a paternalistic and sententious tone, he tried to reassure us. He spoke about our youth and our freedom to live our lives to their fullest. He said we had to devote ourselves to the building of this new society and that he was ready to help us do so. All we had to do in return was sign a statement that would automatically divorce us from our husbands. Such moral bankruptcy! None of the young women in the room agreed to the offer. We all preferred to confront the difficulties that would follow our refusal. When I returned home, I told my father about what had happened in the judge's chambers. I'll never forget his reply: "You must never harm a man who cannot defend himself. I'm proud of your decision!"

We were allowed to see our husbands that same afternoon. The meeting between my husband and our little girl, who had already begun to walk, was overwhelming.

A month later, I was notified that my husband had been transferred to Belene, where he would finish his prison sentence. I was also told that I had the right to send him a ten-kilo package of food, a ten-kilo package of fruit, and a letter once every three months. A visit every three months was also permitted.

The trip to Belene was extremely difficult. The train from Sofia left at noon, and it was toward eleven o'clock at night that I arrived in Svishtov. I spent the night in the train station, and the next morning, at five o'clock, I took a local train that brought me to Belene three hours later. Wagons waited at the station to take us to the camp, which was a good distance away. When I arrived at Belene the first time, I was very surprised to discover that the wagon drivers didn't speak to the families of the inmates. Only afterward did I learn that the locals were forbidden to fraternize in any way with the visitors. They avoided us like the plague. This was the result of fears long cultivated among these people.

The road from the train station led to a tall gate across which were emblazoned the inevitable ideological phrases: "Hail to the Soviet Communist Party," "Long Live the Bulgarian Communist Party," "Forward with Communism," and so forth. To the gate's right rose a watchtower followed by a brick wall. On the other side of the gate were a few barracks. We had to line up in front of one of them and wait hours for a "comrade" to open a small window and take down the names of the inmates who had visitors. We were then taken down a long alley with tall brick walls rising up on either side. At the end of the alley was another tall wall with a small door, in front of which stood a long low table that looked like a workbench. There wasn't a single tree or a single bench. In rain, snow, wind, or hot sun, that is where we waited the entire day. The oldest visitors would lie down and rest on the packed dirt, while children ran here and there. The youngest men ran to the train station to bring back water in bottles and pitchers. Many of the visitors were peasants. All of those who resisted, who refused to surrender their land and livestock and join a cooperative, were interned in the camp.

Toward four o'clock, the door opened and groups of policemen entered the yard. Some of them were carrying metal pins, others a heavy scale, which they placed on the table before setting about their "work." If you could have seen the zeal and pleasure they showed in carrying out their duties! They were in their element: they weighed, took what items they wished from the packages, threw out the fruit, plunged their pins into the jars, broke the loaves of bread and cakes into small pieces, then threw it all back into the bags. They'd swear and curse as they went about their work, and we watched in silence, too afraid to reply. You see, they could cancel the visit! The policemen would then carry inside the verified bags. They next turned to the clothing: they tore open collars and pockets, removed the soles of shoes, all accompanied by the same stream of vulgar, disgusting comments. Once they finished their inspection and took the clothing, the policemen left the yard. We continued to wait with our hearts in our throats. Would they lead in the inmates? Were we going to see them? Were they still alive? It would happen that a policeman would appear, cry out the name of an inmate, and solemnly announce, "He's dead. Here are his clothes!" He'd then toss a bundle of clothing to his family.

The moment of the long-awaited visit would finally arrive. Overcome by anxiety and holding our breaths, we walked through the small door. Groups of seven or eight were let in one at a time. There were two rows of bars that faced one another across a short distance. The inmates stood behind the set of bars at the rear of the room, while we pressed against the bars erected on the side by the door. In the middle stood a policeman as straight as a ramrod for the length of the entire visit, which lasted between five and ten minutes. For three months I lived for these few minutes. There were so many things I wanted to share with the man I loved, but I forgot everything the moment I saw him. I was so upset that I couldn't even speak.

At night, I'd take the local train back to the station at Svichtov, where I'd again spend the night. The next morning, I'd get on the train back to Sofia. And this is how I spent the first few years, making the same awful trip every three months.[5]

During this same time, I completed my studies. They tried to kick me out of the university several times, but I was protected by my colleagues and professors. Since I was married to "an enemy of the people," I couldn't find a job. I took the national exams several times, but despite my excellent results, I was never offered a post. It was only after the condemnation of the Stalinist "cult of personality" that I was able to work as a librarian.

YULIA GURKOVSKA

I was still very small when my family began following my father, who was an inmate, from camp to camp.[6] Obviously, I don't

---

5. Another inmate's wife recounts, "I often went to Belene to see my husband. Then, one day, my husband asked me not to visit again. 'I don't want you to come anymore, because the policeman who accompanies me is on horseback and I'm forced to run alongside.' And it's true, I am the witness: one was on a horse, and the other ran ahead of him. This is why my husband said, 'Don't come again: these visits are too hard'" (*The Survivors*).

6. This section is extracted from the documentary film *The Survivors*.

remember very much from those years, but I still have a few images deeply embedded in my memory. It's winter, and a caravan of wagons is crossing the plains of Dobrudzha. It's very cold. I guess there's a strong wind because the wagon drivers have taken pity and wrapped us with their horse blankets. And in the carriages, there are mostly women, children, and the elderly. I'm with my mother, brother, and grandfather—the father of my father. We were allowed to visit my father at the camp of Nozharevo. I've a vague recollection of seeing a mosque appear in the darkness (night had already fallen, which means that we must have traveled the entire day), where we come to stop. A very old bearded man steps out, falls to his knees, and prays. He then stands up and tells us that Allah excuses him for allowing women to spend the night inside the mosque. He leads us inside and we lie down on the floor.

What I next remember is arriving at the camp. All I recall is a barracks in which there are, against both walls, long benches on which people are seated. We enter, and a man stands up in front of me. He's very skinny and dressed in rags. His face is twisted and badly shaved. He cries, "Yulia!" And ... and he runs toward me to take me in his arms. I stop and push him away, saying that he isn't my father. A deathly silence follows. He then starts to speak, describing our apartment and telling me how I was when I was a baby and how we played together. But I keep pushing him away and telling him, "No, you're not my papa. My papa is handsome and wears a white suit and a hat. You're not my papa."

I didn't allow him to touch me for the entire visit. And I remember that an aged man who had been watching us began to sob. Many people must have cried in this room, but I still wouldn't let my father touch me. Many years later my mother told me that this old man said to her, "Madame, I fought in two wars, but I do not remember ever having cried like that."

I was a little pigheaded monster who wouldn't recognize that ... that it was my father, whose photo moreover I had above my bed at home. And, the truth of the matter is that he was very handsome. Certainly the most handsome of all fathers.

I was overwhelmed not long ago when I went to a meeting of

the survivors of Belene. I nearly suffocated from pain and outrage when I heard the shocking details of everyday life in the camp—details that can never be forgotten but that I never heard my father recount. And I remember that he was a wise man, because these are things I'd never be able to forget. And I'd become spiteful, never living my own life, because I'd be living his instead. I'd never have been able to live the way I do now if I he'd told me these details. And I'm so grateful to him. But I never suspected it was so terrible at Belene. To make a long story short, my father, according to his reckoning, spent ten years, seven months, and twenty-two days at Belene. But he told me only funny stories about his experience: how they'd make fun of a guard or how so-and-so was so silly. Or he'd make me laugh with jokes. He told me stories filled with friendships and beautiful things.

Index